The KINGS TREASURIES
OF LITERATURE

GENERAL EDITOR
Sir A·T·QUILLER COUCH

ATHENA PARTHENOS
IN THE NATIONAL MUSEUM ATHENS

NEW YORK E·P·DUTTON AND COMPANY

THERAS
THE STORY OF AN ATHENIAN BOY
BY CAROLINE DALE SNEDEKER

INTRODUCTION BY
GUY N. POCOCK

All rights reserved

SOLE AGENT FOR SCOTLAND
THE GRANT EDUCATIONAL CO. LTD.
GLASGOW

PRINTED IN GREAT BRITAIN

TO THE
TWO DEAREST CHILDREN
CAROLINE DALE STILWELL
AND
OWEN PARKE MAIER

INTRODUCTION

WHEN, as a boy, one was told for the first time the story of the ancient Greeks, the wonderful men of Attica, a little country no bigger than Yorkshire; when one learnt of the Victory of Marathon won against tremendous odds; of the crushing of the Persian Fleet at Salamis; of the lovely city of Athens with its temples and statues—such statues as the world has never since seen; of their poets and playwrights; their historians and philosophers; their athletes and their orators; one was filled with wonder, but at the same time a sense of aloofness— as if one were reading of a marvellous race living on another planet. It is the same with the Spartans— that blunt, hard people who deliberately gave up all luxury and pleasure and family life in order to produce a race of soldiers perfect in body and brave almost beyond belief. As a boy one thrilled at the story of the defence of the Pass of Thermopylæ; but somehow one never realised that the Spartan boy was no more than a very hardy type of Boy Scout; that the Athenian boy was an ordinary schoolboy like oneself.

The charm of this little book lies in the fact that it breaks through the sense of distance and aloofness. When one reads it one lives again the schoolboy's life in Athens. One can join with the boy Theras in the games and the classes; one may walk the streets and visit the market-place; or climb the marble steps of the Akropolis and see in all its beauty that most lovely building in all the world, the Parthenon. One sees the soldiers with their black tossing plumes—the great galleys, their long oars lashing the water in time to the helmsman's shout—the callous slave-market, where boys were bought and sold; and though it all happened so far away, so long ago, it seems as though the city of Athens, with its bustling streets, its noisy harbour at the end of the Long Walls, had taken life once more—and Theras is as real a boy as the boy who lives next door to us.

Sad times fall upon the home of Theras; his splendid father is killed in war—or so it is reported—and the boy is sent to Sparta. There in that rough and terribly efficient military school he grows lithe and strong—he learns to endure—but he never adopts the Spartan outlook, nor forgets his beloved city of Athens.

At length he determines to escape from the cruel Spartan system and return to his own city. Taking with him a boy of the Perioikoi, the race that inhabited Southern Greece before the coming of the Spartan, he makes his way northwards over desolate mountains and through wild woods—till at length, after enduring great hardships, the boys fall in with Herodotus the great story-teller and historian, and by him are taken back to Athens, where Theras finds his father alive and well, and the family is reunited.

Just the story of a boy, very much like an English

boy of the present day; yet through this story one can visualise the glory that was Greece. The very spirit of Athens is here,—her culture, her vivid daily life, and her marvellous works. And now and then we catch a glimpse of her great men—Pericles, who has given his name to that great age; Herodotus the traveller and historian, whose books still delight the world. One realises, too, that Sparta, for all her courage and sacrifice, has left no lasting monument to the world beyond a few brave names, because her ideals were founded on Violence, while those of Athens were based on true Vision.

G. N. P.

CONTENTS

PART I.—ATHENS

CHAP.		PAGE
I.	Seven Years Old	15
II.	A Walk in the City	17
III.	At School	20
IV.	Learning	23
V.	Athletics	24
VI.	Another Race	26
VII.	Theras tells about it	29
VIII.	The Potter's Wheel	30
IX.	Two Brave Men	32
X.	Climbing the Akropolis	34
XI.	The Goddess Athena	36
XII.	On the Akropolis	38
XIII.	The Goddess of Health	39
XIV.	How Theras ran away	41
XV.	For the Goddess who had no Gifts	45
XVI.	The Parthenon Temple	47
XVII.	The Friendly Toy-Man	48
XVIII.	The Cruel Toy-Man	50
XIX.	The Rescue	53
XX.	The Homecoming	56
XXI.	The Splendid Soldier	57
XXII.	The Slave Market	60
XXIII.	The Father's Going	63
XXIV.	The Right Door	67
XXV.	A Dark Day	68
XXVI.	A Darker Day	70

PART II.—SPARTA

XXVII.	The Old Man Hippias	75
XXVIII.	The Last Sight of Athens	77
XXIX.	Rivals in the Games	80
XXX.	The Robbers' Rocks	81

11

CHAP.		PAGE
XXXI.	Surprise by Night	84
XXXII.	On Guard now	86
XXXIII.	The Spartan Way	89
XXXIV.	A Ship on Land	91
XXXV.	Sparta is so Different from Athens	94
XXXVI.	At Last—Sparta!	95
XXXVII.	Spartan Boys are Soldiers	99
XXXVIII.	Getting used to it	102
XXXIX.	Homesick	105
XL.	The Artemis Victor	109
XLI.	A Shepherd Boy	111
XLII.	The Perioikoi of Sparta	115
XLIII.	A Strange Arrest	118
XLIV.	A Youth too Brave	120
XLV.	Platanistos	123
XLVI.	A Cruel Deed	126

PART III.—A TOUGH JOURNEY

XLVII.	In the Haystacks	131
XLVIII.	The Parting	133
XLIX.	In Taygetos Mountains	136
L.	In the Night	139
LI.	The Spartans Pursue	142
LII.	Forest Journeys	146
LIII.	A Prayer to Pan	150
LIV.	Not a Pussy-Cat	152
LV.	Kindness in Arkadia	155
LVI.	A Dangerous Inn	157
LVII.	A Wilderness	160
LVIII.	The Burden upon Theras	163
LIX.	A Sorrowful Pass	165
LX.	Herodotos	169
LXI.	The Man who knew all the Wonders of the World	172
LXII.	The Bay of Salamis	174
LXIII.	Coming Home	176
LXIV.	Strangers Everywhere	179
LXV.	Real Home	183
LXVI.	The Owl Mark	187
LXVII.	Good-bye	189

PART I.—ATHENS

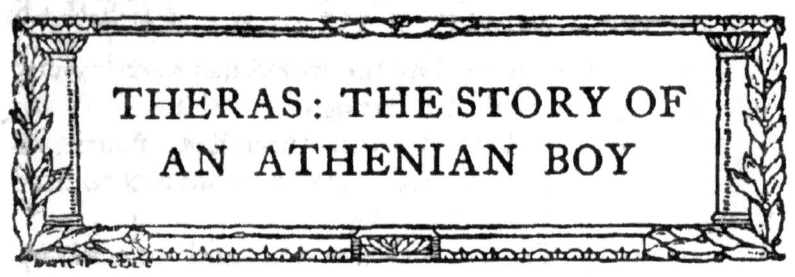

THERAS: THE STORY OF AN ATHENIAN BOY

PART I.—ATHENS

CHAPTER I

Seven Years Old

THERAS was seven years old, and because he was seven he was to go to school. For that was the custom in the city in which he lived. It was an exciting day for everybody in the house, most of all for Theras. For until this time he had had to stay at home with his mother and the servants, and was allowed to play only in the house or in the street close by the front door. Now he was to go out to school with the other boys. Now he would often be with his father and would go to and fro in the city. He already felt grown up.

To go to and fro in the city was what Theras prized. For he lived in the most beautiful city in the world.

It was not such a big city. Everybody knew everybody else, and who were his father and mother and cousins. Nor was it so very rich. Theras's father lived in a plain, simple house, and all his family and cousins lived simply too. But in this city were the wisest and most famous men that the world has ever known, and the most beautiful buildings.

It was called Athens. And though it flourished many years ago, no people since then have been able to make so lovely a city.

No wonder Theras was excited and danced up and down.

"Isn't it time to go?" he said. "Isn't it time to go?"

His mother looked at him wistfully. Glad as she was to have him go she knew she would miss him sorely. For in Athens when once a boy went to school he began to be part of the city life. He was no longer of the house.

"Yes, it is time," she said.

Now into the room came Pheidon, Theras's father, bringing with him a tall man named Lampon.

"Lampon is to be your pedagogue," said Pheidon, and Theras ran to the man, who laughed proudly and took the boy's hand.

"Mind, Lampon, you mustn't be too easy with the boy," said Pheidon. "You are pedagogue now."

By that he meant that Lampon was to take Theras to school, carry his wax tablet which was his writing pad, his stylus (or pencil), and his lyre which was his harp. Lampon was to see that no harm came to Theras, and if necessary he must punish him. Even a boy of fourteen or fifteen in Athens would have his pedagogue.

Lampon was a slave. That means, of course, that Pheidon had bought him in the market just as you would buy a horse or a cow. Lampon was a white man not unlike the Greeks themselves. All people in the whole world bought slaves in those days. The only difference was that the Athenians were kinder to their slaves than were other people. Lampon had been in the house before Theras was born. He loved his master, Pheidon, and his mistress; but his "little master," Theras, he adored, and indeed he was most likely to spoil him.

"Look, Theras, here is your lyre," said his father, and handed him the beautiful little Greek harp. It had bright strings and under the strings was a picture of the god Apollo playing. Every boy must have a new lyre the day he went to school.

"Is it mine?" cried Theras unbelievingly. "My very own?"

He held it out to his little sisters standing near, and when Opis plucked the strings with her baby fingers the harp gave forth a thin sweet sound.

CHAPTER II

A Walk in the City

But now they must start. Theras's mother put on him his long outdoor cloak; for in the house he wore only one garment, like a shirt, reaching to his knees. She also put on his sandals, for he was barefoot. Then Aglaia and Opis, his two little sisters, kissed him. His mother kissed him. You might have thought he was going miles away.

Now his father took his hand, for this being the first day he wanted to take the boy to the schoolmaster himself. Out they went into the bright sunshine, Lampon, the pedagogue, following them. The streets were very narrow in Athens and the houses had no windows, so they seemed to be walking between two high walls with doors in them. The Athenians did not build stately houses for themselves, but only for their gods. The streets were crooked and turned this way and that. It would be easy to get lost.

But high over the city they could see the rocky hill called the Akropolis with the marble temples which Athens had instead of churches. These temples were painted red, blue, and gold and had winged, dragon-like creatures on the roof corners. They looked wonderfully bright up there in the sunshine.

"Father," said Theras, "take me to the Akropolis. I am quite old enough to go to the Akropolis."

"I'll take you, never fear," said his father, "but to-day you are going to school."

Suddenly they came into the bright open space of the market, noisy, bustling, full of life and colour. "Buy my flowers," the flower girls were calling. And all that part of the market bloomed with their pretty wares. "Buy my himations," bawled a great fellow who had white and purple cloaks for sale. "Buy my toys," yelled another who had balls and tiny carts and gilded nuts on his booth. It was the noisiest place Theras had ever seen; and how he loved the noise! Over on one side was a long colonnade, a row of marble pillars roofed like a porch, and with a wall on its farther side. On this wall were painted pictures of warriors taking the city of Troy. Also women warriors on horseback charging upon men who were fighting them with spears.

Theras had never seen a picture-book, and these were the most wonderful pictures he had ever seen. Indeed men journeyed for days over rough roads and rough seas to behold these paintings by Polygnotus.

"Father, stop! Oh, do wait a moment," pleaded Theras. But his father only paused to buy two dolls of baked clay for the small sisters at home, and then they hurried on.

"The market is no place for boys," he said.

"Hail, Pheidon," called a friend, "where are you going so fast?"

"I'm taking my son to school," answered Pheidon proudly.

As they came out again among the narrow streets another friend, Epikides, greeted them.

"Come up to the Pnyx, Pheidon. Phidias is going to speak to us all about buying new ships."

"I will certainly come," said Pheidon, "but first I must take my son to school."

"Your son! How fine!" exclaimed Epikides who had only daughters in his house.

Theras felt his father clasp his hand more tightly. What a lovable, bright world it was!

CHAPTER III

AT SCHOOL

THEY reached the school. It was a little place with only about thirty boys in it; for there were many different schools in Athens, and all were small. They usually consisted of one large room, but this one was a wide porch open to the sunshine with a room to one side where the pedagogues sat waiting for their charges.

The Athenians had everything in the open air—schools, law courts, theatres, everything. The sun shone almost every day of the year. Their sunshine and open-air life made them very healthy and happy people.

On the wall of the school hung the lyres of the boys, the tablets, and the cloaks. The boys sat on benches and the teacher faced them. He was a grim-looking man. Theras was sure he could give a whipping when it was deserved, and perhaps when it was not.

The teacher frowned down on Theras.

"Can your boy sing?" he asked Pheidon.

"Well, I taught him the skolion of Harmodios and Aristogeiton," answered Pheidon. "That was a year ago. He's just a boy. He loves to romp and play."

Now it was very important in Athens for a boy to sing. For if he could sing he could get into one of the boy choruses. That meant he would march in the

AT SCHOOL

processions on holiday festivals, and the father of such a boy would say, "Yes, my boy is in the chorus of Dionysos" or "the chorus of Apollo."

Perhaps the chorus would win the prize for the best singing. Then all the family would be proud. Even Athens itself considered that the boys had done honour to the city.

Therefore the master asked first of all, "Can he sing?"

"But I *can* sing, Father," said Theras in his high, distinct voice. "I know the whole story of Telemachus going to sea."

The boys all nudged each other and giggled. How silly the new boy was, to be sure!

"Silence!" thundered the master. "Theras, if you can sing, sing it. Klinias, you play the lyre."

And Theras, only thinking that he must do the best he could, began at once.

He sang the story—quite a long one, too—of the boy Telemachus in far-away Ithaca whose father, Odysseus, had been wandering the sea for many years. Wicked men thinking his father was dead came into the house and took everything they wanted, ate up all the food, and frightened the boy's mother, Penelope. This troubled Telemachus greatly. What could he do —a boy—among a company of wicked men?

Then the dear goddess Athena came to Telemachus in the likeness of a tall man and talked to the boy about his father. Telemachus, encouraged by her words, went down to the shore and got a ship. He persuaded many honest young men to go with him, and when the sun was set and all the ways were darkened, they slipped away secretly in the ship. Telemachus was going over the sea to find Odysseus, his father.

Theras sang all this in his high, clear voice, sometimes not fitting the words properly to the notes, but singing in time and very earnestly. As he finished he leaped toward his father, crying out:

"And oh, Father, if you were lost on the sea, I'd take a boat and come out to find you, no matter if it took me years and years."

"Theras, Theras," said Pheidon, "how did you learn that song?"

"I heard you sing it," said the boy.

"But I never sang it for you."

"No, but when you have a feast in the aula I come down and listen at the door. That is how I learn."

"But you are in bed."

"I jump out of bed," said Theras, laughing.

Now, of course, it was disobedient of Theras to come down to his father's feasts when he was supposed to be fast asleep, but Pheidon was so pleased with what the boy had learned that he could not scold him.

However, the master noted it and determined to watch Theras sharply and punish him if he did not obey.

CHAPTER IV

LEARNING

THEN Pheidon went away and school began. It must have been easy learning. They had no history, no geography, no drawing, no language except their own language, the Greek. They must learn to read and write, to play the lyre and sing poems. The poems were all from the two great poems of Homer.

One of these poems, the *Iliad*, was the story of an army of Greek fighting men who went across the sea. They had breathless adventures. When they reached Troy there was great fighting with the Trojans and many were killed. The boys loved the story. Two of the older boys knew the whole *Iliad* by heart. This was like knowing the whole New Testament by heart, but as the boys had little else to do, many a boy in the city learned to do that much.

The very morning Theras came, a big boy named Perimedes recited, or rather sang (for they always sang it), the whole story of the Wooden Horse. Theras grew so excited that he could hardly sit still in his seat. Now he kicked his feet against the bench, now he sat perfectly still leaning forward to listen.

When the story was finished Theras had to write on his tablet. This was a little square board covered with smooth wax. To write upon it you had to scratch it with a sharp point. The master wrote "A B G," which is the Greek "A B C," or rather, Alpha, Beta, Gamma, Delta, for they did not say their alphabet just as we do. Theras tried and tried, but he scratched the whole face of his tablet without making one good letter. Then the master held the tablet over burning charcoal, warmed it, and smoothed it all fair again. This was like washing a slate to begin anew. Then he rapped Theras's knuckles with his stick and told him he must do it right. So this time, beginning very carefully, Theras wrote his "A B G."

He was very glad when lunch-time came, for his back was aching from sitting on the hard bench.

CHAPTER V

Athletics

For lunch the boys ate cheese and bread and honey cakes. Then came the fun of marching through the city, all of them together, to the athletic field. Each boy walked with his pedagogue. All wore their long cloaks, or himations, and walked quickly with downcast eyes. Some of the older boys were splendid fellows, and often the men they passed would notice them.

"Look at Perimedes," they would whisper. "They say he is famous at the long jump. He will jump at the Olympic Games next year."

And another man would say:

"There's Klinias. He won a prize at Delphi playing

ATHLETICS

the lyre and singing. And Telamon yonder, he's the fastest runner of his age in Athens."

The boys blushed at this, and their pedagogues hustled them along so that they would not hear the praise and become vain.

They passed out of the city and onward to a shady grove of olive trees. Here was a running track and some little mounds from which the boys would leap.

As soon as the boys saw these they gave a great shout. They kicked off their sandals, threw off their himations and chitons. Then they were stripped ready for their exercise. They were brown as berries, every one of them, tanned all over by the sun as most boys are tanned on neck and arms after the summer at the seashore.

The gymnastic teacher, "gymnasiarch," they called him, was waiting.

"Come, Klinias and Telamon," he said. "You are to run a race to-day."

Now Theras had taken a fancy to Klinias. He was a handsome boy with a free-and-easy way about him. Whenever Theras had looked up during the morning he had found Klinias ready to smile at him in friendly fashion. When the other boys laughed at Theras, Klinias did not laugh. Now he stood with Telamon with foot on the line, stooping, ready for the word.

"Ready! Go!" called the gymnasiarch, and off they flew down the track. How their brown heels twinkled in the sunshine. The dust rose behind them.

Poor Klinias! Of course he could not win against

Telamon. Had not those men said that Telamon was the best runner in Athens? The boys tore the air with yells.

"Telamon, Telamon!"

"Go it, Telamon!"

"Ho! *Klinias!* Look at Klinias! By Hermes, look at him!"

Sure enough, Klinias had come up even with Telamon. On, on they flew, shoulder to shoulder.

Theras shouted wildly, lost his breath. Then shouted again. Now Klinias shot ahead. Theras began to dance up and down. There was Klinias at the goal! Ho! Klinias! Klinias!

"He's been practising like anything lately," the boys were saying to each other. "Think of it! Beat Telamon!"

Theras was so happy he could only keep shouting, "Klinias, Klinias!" until one of the boys said:

"Listen to little Whiteback." They called him this because he was not tanned like the rest. Theras resolved to stay out in the sun every moment until he should grow as brown as Klinias.

CHAPTER VI

Another Race

"Come, boys," said the gymnasiarch. "Each to your own work. You younger boys come throw the disc."

The disc was a round bronze plate. Each boy

ANOTHER RACE

threw it in turn. He would stoop, holding the disc low; then with a short, quick run and a glorious swing of the right arm, send it flying. A pedagogue marked with a spear where each disc fell.

All this was new to Theras. Each time his turn came his disc fell short of the shortest throw.

"Oh, Whiteback, Whiteback, now watch Whiteback!"

"A cat could throw as well as that. A hen could, a chicken! A chicken just out of its shell!" The boys jeered until Theras could hardly throw at all.

After this the younger boys had to run up the little mounds and leap off. This was a great contest. But here, too, Theras's leap was the poorest of all, and every try he made brought him a chorus of laughs and jeers. Theras felt like crying, but of course he did not let anybody see how he felt.

"Now you are to run races, you younger boys," ordered the gymnasiarch. "Theras, you and Dryas and Koretas run first."

Suddenly Klinias was at his side.

"Look here, Theras," he said in a low voice, "haven't you ever practised running?"

"Oh, yes," answered Theras. "Lampon showed me how. I practise almost every day."

"You look as if you could run," said Klinias. "Those two boys the master has put against you are the poorest runners in the school. You ought to beat them if you try."

"Come now, hurry," called the gymnasiarch, and in an instant the three boys stood with feet on the mark.

"On your mark! Ready! Set! Go!"

With a leaping heart Theras sprang forward. He knew he must save his strength at first and run steadily. He kept his eyes on the goal.

"Klinias says I can win. I can." He did not say this, but something inside of him kept saying it for him. He ran abreast with Dryas, but Koretas was still ahead.

Theras had not really tried yet. He was neither winded nor tired. He loved to run.

"Great Hermes," he thought suddenly, "there is the goal. Now I must spring."

And with one push he shot far ahead of Koretas.

"Ho, Whiteback! Whiteback!" yelled the boys, but Theras did not hear them. He was too busy running.

"By Zeus, well done, well done," said the gymnasiarch, patting him on the back. "A second Pheidon."

Theras knew what he meant; for his father, Pheidon, had won the running race at Olympia before Theras was born.

Klinias came running up.

"I knew you could do it!" he cried delightedly. "You've got the legs and the grit."

Surely Klinias was the most wonderful boy in the world.

THERAS TELLS ABOUT IT

CHAPTER VII

THERAS TELLS ABOUT IT

AFTER their practice each boy had a cold shower under the fountain and the pedagogues rubbed them all down. Then, glowing warm, they put on their clothes again and walked back to the city.

"Your father said you might give these to your sisters," said Lampon, giving Theras the two dolls which Pheidon had bought in the market.

The little girls were waiting in the aula, the sitting room of the house, an open court which had no roof. They came running with outstretched arms. They were so delighted with the dolls that they did not think to ask about school.

But his mother, Arethusa, asked, and Theras began to talk just as fast as he could.

"Oh, Mother, I wrote on the tablet——

"Oh, Mother, I ran a race——

"Oh, Mother, there's a boy named Klinias——"

All through the supper he talked. Just as if a little bell were being shaken till its clapper tinkled all the time—so went Theras's tongue.

But the minute he had taken the last bite, his eyes drooped and he began to nod.

"I think I'll go to bed," he said. "I'm not exactly sleepy, but I must be up at five o'clock to go to school."

The last part of this sentence was true. School began early in Athens.

CHAPTER VIII

THE POTTER'S WHEEL

ONE day as Theras and Lampon were coming from school, whom should they meet but Pheidon.

"What, home so early?" asked the father.

"Yes, it's a half-holiday," answered Theras.

"All right," said Pheidon, laughing, "you shall spend it with me."

They were in the Street-of-the-Marble-Workers where everybody was making statues. *Clink, clink, clink*—you heard the hammers everywhere.

Pheidon led him out of this and into the Kerameikos or Potters' Quarter. Here he stopped before a shop which was open all along the front of it. What fun it was to see the man squatting at his wheel and making a pot out of soft clay!

The wheel, made of solid wood (no spokes), lay flat before him like a table, and all the while the potter kept whirling, whirling it. Then he slapped down a handful of clay on the middle of the wheel and smoothed the whirling mass into a round shape.

With both hands the potter pressed its sides, and it grew tall; then he put one fist in the middle, and it grew hollow. All the time it quivered and trembled. The clay certainly seemed alive.

"Oh, look, look!" cried Theras. "It's beginning to be a vase."

Already it had a base and a pretty slender neck. Then the man squeezed it boldly.

"Oh, Father, he's spoiled it," cried Theras.

The potter smiled.

"Do you think so, little master?" he asked, and with one more touch he changed it into a pitcher.

Surely that was magic!

Behind the potter stood many vases drying on shelves.

In the next booth was a big oven with flaming red wood fire under it. Pheidon told Theras that vases were baking in the oven as though they were so many cakes.

Farther along the street they came to a shop of finished vases painted black. A painter with a fine brush was drawing outline pictures upon the red clay vase. Afterwards he would paint all the background black, leaving the figures red. To Theras it was like a story-book. For there was Telemachus getting into his boat and the goddess Athena standing at the prow to help him. And on the other side of the vase Telemachus had already reached Sparta and was asking old Nestor if he had seen Odysseus anywhere.

"Oh, Father, buy me that vase," said Theras.

"You mustn't want everything you see," answered Pheidon firmly. "I am going to buy that big jar over yonder for Mother."

This was huge, as tall as Theras, and wide-throated. It had only a black border and no pictures.

"What do you suppose Mother will do with it?" asked Pheidon.

"She'll keep grain in it to make flour for us," answered Theras, and strange to say, he was right.

CHAPTER IX

Two Brave Men

It was a good two weeks before Pheidon could keep his promise to his son and take him to the Akropolis. Pheidon was a very busy man, and yet he really had no business. No full Athenian citizen had any business, or work of money getting, to do. To be sure, Pheidon owned a good farm at the foot of Hymettos Mountain and he owned several ships. But the farm was worked by slaves and a faithful slave superintended it. Pheidon went once a week to see it. His two ships were sailed by two shipmasters who were paid by Pheidon for doing it. Yet Pheidon worked. All his work was for the city, and for it he got no pay. This year he was judge. He must decide fairly all the disputes which came before him, for if he did not decide wisely he could be punished for his failure when his term was up.

Pheidon was also paying for the training of a chorus which would sing at the next festival, and he was helping to train it in singing. When the boys would sing, everybody in Athens would hear and enjoy the music.

Above all Pheidon was a soldier, and had to practise running and wrestling every day, so that if Athens went to war he could fight for her. Greek fighting was all hand to hand. The strong, quick man was the best soldier.

Pheidon loved all these duties. His work was his great pleasure. He was busy all day long.

But early one bright morning he came to Theras.

"Theras," he said, "put on your sandals and your himation. This morning we go to the Akropolis. My good ship *Daphne* has come back safe to land. I am going to thank Athena."

Soon they were out among the winding and interesting streets. At every corner and turn was a statue. In front of every door was a curious Apollo statue (Apollo Aguieus they were called) to guard the house and keep the folk inside from harm.

Presently in an open space they came upon statues of two men beside each other leaping forward with their swords.

"Oh, Father, are they alive?" asked Theras foolishly. For they were painted in living colours.

"Don't you know them?" asked his father. "Harmodios and Aristogeiton?"

Sure enough, they were the ones about whom Theras had sung the little song, or skolion, when he was only six years old. They had lived long ago when Athens had had a terrible king. The king, called the Tyrant, would allow no one to vote. He made all the laws himself and everyone had to obey him. To the Athenians this was a dreadful thing. For they loved to be free, just as we do.

The two young men, Harmodios and Aristogeiton, hid their swords in myrtle boughs which they carried for the festival, and standing at this very corner, sprang out and killed the Tyrant. They themselves

B

were instantly killed by the Tyrant's guard. But all Athens was free again.

"Oh, yes—yes, I know them," answered Theras, and at once he began to sing in his strong, clear voice:

> "In a myrtle bough shall my sword be hid.
> This Harmodios and Aristogeiton did,
> The day they struck the Tyrant down
> And made our Athens a free man's town."

All the way Theras kept singing and humming to himself, "a free man's town, a free man's town."

CHAPTER X

Climbing the Akropolis

INDEED, Theras's very heart was singing this morning. He was so happy that he did not walk, but kept skipping and leaping along at his father's side. If the schoolmaster had been there he would surely have punished him.

Now the Akropolis rose up close before them and seemed to reach the sky. They began to climb it.

The Akropolis is not just a hill. It is one solid, big rock with cliffs like the sides of a house, and it is flat on top like a table. Only the front side of it slants, and here are marble steps.

As Pheidon and Theras mounted, the air grew fresher and sweeter. The winds from the mountains blew upon them.

CLIMBING THE AKROPOLIS

"Look back now," said Pheidon. "There's our city."

Sure enough they could see the houses as small as toys and the streets winding among them. Around it a wall enclosed the city as though it were in a nest.

This wall made Athens safe. No one had guns or cannons in those days. Fighting was done with swords, spears, arrows and slings. So when at night the great gates of Athens were closed, no one could hurt Athens.

They climbed higher. They could see the plain and the farms beyond the city, the groves of olive trees. Olive leaves are grey, so that a grove of them seen from above looks like grey, shimmering silk.

Beyond the eastern plains rose a splendid mountain, dark blue now, the colour of a ripe plum. At the top was a rim of red; for the sun was rising beyond it.

"Oh, see, see Hymettos," cried Theras, "and the rosy-fingered dawn. Good-morning, Honey Mountain."

He called it Honey Mountain because Hymettos's slopes were full of bees and almost all the honey came from Hymettos. There was no sugar in those days. All Theras's cakes and candy were sweetened with honey. Now if you have never eaten honey candy I beg you to make some. It's so much sweeter and more delicious than sugar candy.

Never was a sea so blue, so blue. And islands were there. Oh, so many of them, lying "like polished shields on the glancing deep." These islands belonged to Athens.

And now—oh, now, they were at the top! There they were among hundreds of statues, painted so that they looked alive, among temples with columns, among all the treasures of Athens.

Right before them stood the goddess Athena herself, giant high, made of bright bronze, five times taller than a mortal man. She wore a helmet on her head, and carried aloft a spear. The sunlight touched the helmet so that it shone like a mirror, and the tip of the spear seemed to be afire.

"Athena, Athena!" cried Theras, stretching up his hands in prayer to her. "My dear goddess."

Shivers of delight ran up and down his back. Pheidon knew that it was only a *statue* of Athena, but to Theras it seemed the goddess herself.

I do not blame him, for so beautiful was this Athena that I would willingly go twice around the world to see her.

CHAPTER XI

The Goddess Athena

The most important person in Athens—by far the most important—was Athena.

She was more important than Pheidon who was a judge, than Euripides who was a great poet, than Pericles who was the most prominent citizen of the city.

"But," you will object, "Athena was not a *person*. She was only a goddess, a sort of myth. How could she be important?"

THE GODDESS ATHENA

She was important because all the people in Athens except a few philosophers believed in her.

To the Athenians she stood in the place of God Himself.

The Athenians thought there were many gods: Zeus, who made the thunder and who owned all the bright sky; Hermes, who had wings on his heels and took you on your journeys; Artemis, the goddess of little girls. Little girls must always give their toys to Artemis when they grew up. There were many gods and goddesses—so the Greeks thought—and each city had a god or goddess all its own.

Athena was the goddess of Athens. She loved Athens more than any other city. Some people even thought she lived in a house on the Akropolis.

Athena was a lovely maiden, taller and more beautiful than any human maid. She wore helmet and breastplate, because when Athenians went to war she always went with them and fought for them. She had grey eyes and the kindest smile in the world.

If you were in trouble Athena might put on her sandals, which never grew old, and come flying through the air to help you. You probably would not recognise her. You would think she was some good friend you knew. You would talk with her and she would advise you and help you. Then all of a sudden "your friend" would be wrapped in a cloud or a rosy mist, and so would disappear. Then you would know you had seen Athena.

All this Theras believed. But you must not think him foolish for so believing. Athena was his goddess.

The wise, grown-up men in Athens believed in her, respected her, and loved her.

And often they prayed to Athena so truly and thought her so good and kind that their prayers reached to the true God over all.

CHAPTER XII

On the Akropolis

WHEN Theras went up on the Akropolis he was in Athena's home. No wonder he thought the tall brazen goddess was Athena herself.

Theras and Pheidon walked past the many statues of gods, and warriors and heroes, statues of boys who had won prizes for running or throwing the disc. They were all painted so that they looked alive. Pheidon and Theras walked straight to the Parthenon, Athena's beautiful temple, for Pheidon must now thank the goddess for bringing his ship back home.

The temple door was to the east, so that the sun could shine in the moment it arose over the mountain. The sun was shining into it now.

Theras caught a gleam and glitter of gold.

"What is it?" he whispered.

Pheidon took his hand and answered in a low, solemn voice:

"It is the new image of Athena, the one Phidias made."

They stepped into the lovely temple. The sunlight from behind them fell straight upon the breast of the image and from there shone in a golden mist upon the face—such a great *thinking* face! It was just the colour of little Opis's face, awakening rosy from sleep. The goddess's grey eyes looked down into Theras's eyes as though she were loving him, really noticing him, and at the same time dreaming about heaven.

"Has she had a dream?" whispered Theras.

Pheidon did not answer, and when Theras looked up he saw tears running down his father's face. Somehow he did not dare to ask why. But doubtless it was for joy that the image was so beautiful. It had just been placed there and was not quite finished. Pheidon had not seen it before.

Then they came out. Pheidon did not remember to tell Theras that the image, which reached the roof of the temple, was made of ivory and gold.

Such an image was called Chryselephantine. *Chrys* means gold. I will leave you to guess why *elephantine* means ivory.

CHAPTER XIII

THE GODDESS OF HEALTH

PHEIDON made his sacrifice at the great altar in front of the temple. Then they were ready to go home.

As they neared the steps again, Theras noticed a

small statue standing beside the path. It leaned forward a little with hands outstretched. An altar was at its feet, but no gifts were on the altar.

"Father," whispered Theras again, "look at the poor little goddess asking for gifts, and no one has given her any!"

Pheidon laughed.

"Oh, no, son!" he said. "She is not asking but giving. That is a statue of Hygeia (Health). Pericles put her here to thank Athena because a slave he loved and who had been very ill grew well again. The slave was working on the Parthenon over there, and fell from a great height and hurt himself so that everybody thought he would die, but after many prayers he grew well again. So Pericles asked Phidias to make this statue of Hygeia giving health."

They had walked by, but Theras ran back again to look.

"No, Father," he said. "No, I think the poor little goddess wants some gifts. I wish we could give her something."

"I have given all my gifts," answered Pheidon.

But all the way down the steps into the town and even after he reached home Theras was thinking, not of the great goddess with the tall spear, nor of the smiling golden goddess in the temple, but rather of little "Health" who stood near the entrance and had no gifts at all.

CHAPTER XIV

How Theras ran away

ONE day when Theras was ten years old his father gave him two drachmas.

As a matter of fact, Pheidon had never before given him money. He thought it better for him to buy whatever his boy might want.

But now Pheidon was going to take Theras to the market, called the Agora, and let him stay a few moments to buy toys for himself. It was a festival time and a holiday from school.

"But, son, I cannot go until to-morrow," he said. "Keep your drachmas carefully until then."

They were such handsome pennies, these drachmas; they had a picture of Athena on one side and an owl on the other, and they were of bright silver. Theras played with them all morning—spinning them, tossing them, and catching them again.

It was old Gorgo, the nurse, who put a new idea into his head, though indeed she did not mean to do so.

"Yes, and ye'll lose 'em both," she said. "Your father should have taken ye to-day to spend 'em. There'll be no drachmas to-morrow!"

"I won't lose them, Gorgo."

"Oh, yes, ye will," answered the nurse. "I know you."

Theras stopped playing. What a terrible thing!

To-morrow would come and there would be no drachmas and no going to market.

Suddenly he thought: "Then I'll go to-day. I'll go by myself."

Of course, he knew this was wrong. No boy was allowed to go to market by himself. His father was very indulgent to take him there even for a few moments.

Theras went slowly out of the house. He thought maybe he would just play by the front door and not go any farther. But when he came out, no one was in sight, and the old slave who always kept the door was talking and not looking at Theras at all.

So Theras walked down the street, at first very slowly and then faster and faster as he grew brave to go alone. Boys were never allowed to go thus about the city. This seems strange to us. But there was good reason, as Theras was to find out before the day was done. He knew the way perfectly by now. Had he not gone to school every day with Lampon?

Soon he was at the Agora. It was full of people, and there was the booth of toys and the funny big man who always stood there bawling:

"Buy my toys, buy my toys,
Nice red balls for girls and boys!"

Theras went up to the booth and picked up a lovely red ball, a large one which even Aglaia could catch.

"It will be as much fun for Aglaia as for me," he thought.

"How much is it?" he asked.

"That there ball, that's the finest in my shop. It cost a drachma."

Theras was delighted that he should get the finest ball on the booth and paid his drachma quickly. The man's eyes sparkled, for the drachma was five times too much for the ball. Theras had never handled money before.

Just then a clear voice spoke out:

"Why, Theras, son of Pheidon, what in the world are you doing here alone in the Agora?"

It was his father's friend, Epikides, looking at him with a most astonished face.

Theras blushed as red as his ball.

"I'm going home now," he said hastily. "Straight home!"

"You'd better," laughed Epikides, and Theras ran across the Agora to the street from which he had come.

But there in the street he saw that he had his ball in his one hand and one drachma in the other. What a shame not to spend both drachmas while he was about it.

Then quite suddenly he thought of that little goddess on the Akropolis, the goddess Hygeia, who stretched out her hands yet had no gifts. What a wonderful thing to buy a barley cake for Hygeia and then—oh—and then to go up to the Akropolis and *give* it to her! Surely his father could not be angry with him for giving gifts to the gods. That was the best act an Athenian could do.

Carefully Theras stole back to the Agora. Epikides

was nowhere to be seen. Theras went over to the cake vendors and found the little flat barley cakes which were made especially for the gods. There was also some powdered myrrh which could be burned on the altar.

The air all about the booth smelled sweet because of the myrrh. The Athenians thought that when the smoke smelling so sweet of myrrh rose up to heaven the gods could sniff it and enjoy it.

"I want two cakes and I want some myrrh," said Theras.

"That's four obols," said the man.

"Would a drachma do?" asked Theras.

"Oh, yes, seeing it's you, little master," said the man with a wink.

Now as it takes six obols to make a drachma, Theras again paid too much. But he was very happy. The man gave him the myrrh in a tiny vase.

The cake-booth was near the colonnade where were the beautiful pictures of Polygnotus. There were the warriors fighting for Troy, just as Perimedes had sung it at school. Now Theras saw all the splendid warriors with long spears. He knew every figure in the pictures. Why should he not?—for their names were written beside each one.

There was Odysseus, the father of Telemachus. Odysseus was making the great wooden horse. Theras would have known him by this even if his name had not been there. The horse was hollow and the warriors climbed into it. Then they gave it as a present to the Trojans.

Theras thrilled with delight when he saw this. He had always wanted to know how Odysseus looked and now here he was—such a splendid warrior with helmet and sword. Pictures were a rare treat to an Athenian boy.

Here Theras glanced around and saw that the toyman was looking at the pictures too. He had sold out his booth and now was taking his pleasure. Theras was glad to see him, but it made him remember that he must go now to the little goddess Health and give his gifts.

So he took a last look at the pictures and hurried away.

CHAPTER XV

For the Goddess who had no Gifts

A BROAD street led out of the Agora straight to the Akropolis, so Theras could not lose his way. Every once in a while as he walked along he took out the vase of myrrh and smelt it. How good it was and how delighted the goddess would be!

Then he folded the cakes and vase close in his cloak. No Athenian boy would go out without his cloak. Even though he was running away, Theras had remembered it.

Now he began to climb the marble steps of the Akropolis as he had done with his father. Theras had no time to look back at the city or Hymettos Mountain, but when he caught sight of the sea he took a long breath. He loved it. All Athenians loved the sea.

Now he was at the top among a very forest of statues. Beyond these the two temples of Athena, the small Erechtheum and the great Parthenon, seemed to smile at him, as though they were glad he had come.

And near at hand right at the entrance stood the little goddess he had come to see, still holding out her hands for gifts.

Theras looked about him bashfully, not knowing what to do.

An altar attendant spoke to him.

"Are you looking for your pedagogue?" he asked.

"No, I have some gifts for the goddess Hygeia and I don't know how to give them."

The attendant wore a short cloak of pure white. His head was crowned with flowers. Theras liked him at once, for he was good to look upon.

"I'll help you," said the man kindly.

He brought some cedar twigs and a lighted torch. Then he put a crown of lovely hyacinth flowers on Theras's head. He laid the twigs on Hygeia's altar and set fire to them with his torch.

"Now, little man," he said, and Theras laid first the myrrh then the cakes upon the flame.

"Do you think she would like my ball, too?" he whispered. "It has been so long since anybody brought her a gift."

"No," said the man gently, "I think she would rather you kept the ball."

Now the sweet smell of the myrrh filled the air.

The blue smoke curled up in the sunshine and reached the very nose of the goddess. Theras was sure he saw her sniff with her nose and smile.

He stood in holy silence, lifting his hands on high and praying to Hygeia to be good to his father, mother, and little sisters.

"And remember me also, Hygeia," he prayed; "because I have brought you these gifts."

And surely some good spirit heard the prayer, for a kind power took care of Theras that day.

CHAPTER XVI

The Parthenon Temple

So the sacrifice was ended and the attendant went away to other duties.

Theras wandered along the way toward the Parthenon. Some men were working on the front of it over the porch, the part called the pediment. They were carving a statue of Apollo. It was unfinished and looked very strange as yet, as if a veil were hiding it. Theras had to guess what the head was, and the hands and feet. There were to be a number of gods over the temple porch seated and talking together.

Theras stood watching the men work and looking at the temple. How bright it was, all red and blue and gold! And how tall and stately the pillars of the porch and the splendid pillars which went all around it. At the eave corners the bronze griffins lifted their wings on high. It looked as if the whole temple might flutter away on their wings.

Theras grew very happy as he lingered, happy and very still. He did not know why, but it was because the beautiful temple was standing there, new and holy in the sunshine.

It was the most beautiful building in the world, and no one could see it without feeling this strange happiness.

And even to-day, when it is two thousand five hundred years old, all broken, with no roof, and the lovely statues of the gods all gone, it is still the most beautiful building in the world, and it still gives that same feeling of happiness to those who look upon it.

CHAPTER XVII

THE FRIENDLY TOY-MAN

SOMEONE touched Theras's shoulder and spoke to him.

"Well, little master, did you come out to see the city?"

Theras looked around. It was the toy-man, the very man who had sold him the ball.

"Yes," answered Theras, "and now I am going home."

"Home already? Why, you have hardly seen anything."

"I've seen the Agora and the Akropolis," insisted Theras.

"Pooh, that's nothing. The day isn't near over. Have ye seen the Piræus, now?"

He pointed down toward the sea to where the little town of Piræus lay along the shore with ships all crowding up to it like bees around a bed of flowers. It was the landing-place for all the ships of Athens.

"My father took me there once to see the ships," said Theras.

"Oh, but I wish you could see the ship that's in the harbour now—*Medusa*. The newest ship in the navy, it is. Just look at the beak on her prow! I tell you, when that beak rams into a ship—it's death to the enemies of Athens!"

"I'll tell Father and he'll take me to-morrow," said Theras eagerly.

"To-morrow! That'll never do. Why, that ship sails away to-night."

Theras's face saddened.

"I'll tell ye," said the man, as if he had just thought of it, "I'll take ye down there if ye like and I'll bring ye home again right to the door."

"Oh, will you?" exclaimed Theras. "Will you?" He thought the man was wonderfully kind to offer this. He did not like to refuse and be impolite. And oh, he did want to go out to that ship—just one more pleasure before he went home. "Yes," he said brightly, "I'll go."

The man took his hand, but Theras quickly slipped

his hand away. The man's fingers were so dirty and seemed all made of knuckles.

However, he walked at the man's side. The man took Theras down some rough, rock-hewn steps at the back of the Akropolis. "A nearer way," he said, and Theras thought it was great fun to go down the little rough steps. Then through strange, narrow streets and along the road between the "Long Walls" which led from Athens to the sea. Theras was tired and hot when they reached the docks at last.

CHAPTER XVIII

THE CRUEL TOY-MAN

THERE, sure enough, was the ship with a great painted dragon at her prow, rearing up fierce, and dancing on the waves as if alive. Underneath, in front of the dragon, was a series of bright metal beaks as sharp as spears.

"Ye see she's got four beaks," said the man.

"I see only three," said Theras.

He forgot all about being tired, the ship was so wonderful.

"Four, I tell ye. Climb right up here and ye can see 'em all."

He helped Theras to the deck of a little boat and pushed off toward the ship.

Nearer and nearer came the great hulk of the

THE CRUEL TOY-MAN 51

Medusa, until she rose bright and red and splendid before their very eyes.

"But you're going *past* it!" cried Theras.

"Only a little way. The wind caught me."

"But then why are you putting up the sail?" asked Theras.

"Oh, there's more things to see," said the man easily.

Strange how small the big ship *Medusa* began to look all of a sudden, and how far, oh, how very far the wharves of the Piræus and how big the sea all about them.

"Where are you going?" cried Theras, frightened.

"Ye keep still now," said the man roughly. "Ye give one scream and I'll hit ye."

Theras was so astonished that for a moment he could only open his mouth. Then he answered, "You won't dare to hit me. I am Pheidon's son."

"Pheidon's son or not, I'll kill ye if ye scream."

Theras was very quick. In a flash he was at the boat's edge, leaping into the sea. He was a good swimmer and he thought he could reach the dock.

But a sailor appeared from nowhere, caught his leg, and dragged him back. Now Theras screamed loud enough, but by this time the boat was too far out for anyone to hear.

The two men tied his hands and feet. Theras fought all the time.

Then the men ran to the sail and tiller.

"Where to?" asked the sailor.

"To Chios," answered the toy-man.

"Oh—oh!" screamed Theras. For he knew that Chios was a little island far out in the sea where slaves were bought and sold. The toy-man was going to sell him as a slave.

For a while Theras kept crying. Then all of a sudden he thought that it did no good to cry. No one could hear or help him. So he lay still and tried to think how he could help himself.

"When the trader of Chios buys me I'll tell him Pheidon of Athens will pay much money for me," he thought.

He knew that his father would sell all his slaves, his ships, and his house to buy back his son. Poor Pheidon!

The long afternoon wore away slowly. The two men cursed the wind because it died down and they could not sail. But they kept a little headway with their long oars. As they rowed they talked of Theras.

"How much do you suppose that boy'll bring?" asked the sailor.

"Oh, I can get two minæ for him. He's a fine, likely boy. He'd be good now running long errands. If I don't sell him at Chios, I'll go over to Ephesus. I know a Persian who comes there to trade."

Theras broke into a cold sweat of fear. He had to catch his breath over and over again to keep from crying. Would he be an errand-boy under some cruel master who would make him run in the hot sun and beat him when the day was over? Or worse still, a Persian's slave? The Persians cut off the ears of a slave who did not obey.

THE RESCUE

Oh, he would never see his father again! He knew how easily these men could hide in some bay of the islands. Pheidon could never trace them. Theras thought of his mother at home, of little Opis asking why he did not come back.

Then the wind came up—*whew!*—and caught the sail, sending them skimming along.

"Good. Praised be Zeus!" cried the toy-man.

Theras turned over to hide his face. He could not help crying now, for he knew they were nearing Chios.

He did not know how long he lay so, for at last he fell asleep.

CHAPTER XIX

THE RESCUE

HE was awakened by the little boat rolling and pitching. The two men were scrambling about, pulling at the sail as if they had lost their wits. Now they prayed to the gods. Now they swore. Theras had never heard such dreadful words.

"Get before the wind, Moira catch you!" shouted the toy-man. "Be quick, she's coming nearer!"

Theras sat up. He could not use his arms, those being tied fast, so he used the strong muscles of his waist as he did in the gymnasium, and sat up quickly.

The sun was setting, a clear red ball. But all the sea was purple, so deep a purple that it seemed it would colour the very boat moving through it. The sky was pink and had little soft pink clouds.

Then Theras saw far off on the sea a big ship with many oars on both sides of it, flashing like whirling wings. It was coming so fast that it grew bigger every moment.

It was the Athenian ship, the very ship, *Medusa*, which Theras had seen at the Piræus.

"O Athena!" he prayed. "Bring the ship to save me! Take me home to Athens—your city!"

Nearer came the *Medusa*. Now he could see the red dragon at her prow. The dragon came forward, dipping and rising, grinning as if in glee that it had found the little boat. Yes, now they were getting ready their ropes.

The long oars as they smote the water made a ripping sound and sent up sparkling spray.

The toy-man with a yell leaped overboard and swam away. But the other man was too frightened to swim.

For by this time the big ship was alongside. The sailors leaped nimbly over into the boat. But quicker than any sailor came Pheidon himself, his father! His father whom Theras thought he should never see again.

"Theras!" cried Pheidon. "My son, my little boy!"

He caught Theras up in his arms. With his sword he cut off the ropes from wrists and ankles. He kissed the ankles because they were bruised and bleeding, and kissed Theras's wrists too. He was crying because he was so glad.

THE RESCUE

Then he climbed swiftly up the rope ladder, holding Theras in one arm.

When he got into the ship he kissed Theras all over again as if he hadn't done it before.

As for Theras, he could only cling to his father and hide his face for joy.

"I ran away," he faltered. "Oh, I'm so sorry, so sorry!"

"The gods have punished you, my boy. I know you won't do it again."

Epikides was there, for he had helped to find Theras.

And now the big ship turned about and began to leap back toward Athens.

"Son, are you hungry?" asked Pheidon.

"Oh, Father, *have* you something to eat?" cried Theras, with such a blissful look that everybody laughed.

Then Pheidon brought out bread and cheese, goat's milk and honey. And never, never had anything tasted so good.

"Oh, Father, I'm so glad you brought it," said Theras, with his mouth full.

"That was Mother's thought," said Pheidon. "Poor Mother!"

Yes indeed, poor Mother! Theras felt more ashamed than ever, for Mother was still waiting miserably at home and did not know.

"Look!" said Pheidon. "There is our Athens!"

Sure enough, there on the sea's edge was the shore like a dark mist of violet above which was a bright, bright gleam like gold. It was the gleam of Athena's spear catching the sunset—that biggest Athena of all who stood outside the temple on the Akropolis and held her spear on high for all sailors to see.

Tears came to the boy's eyes as he saw it.

"Oh, Father," he whispered, "I might never have seen Athens again."

"My son," said Pheidon solemnly, "if Epikides had not passed by you in the Agora, you certainly would never have seen Athens again."

And Theras caught his breath for fear and gladness.

CHAPTER XX

The Homecoming

At the door Mother was waiting to receive them. How she laughed and cried and then laughed again for joy! She looked very pale, as if she had been ill for a long time. Little Aglaia and Opis danced around, wondering why everybody should be so astonished to see Theras when he had been gone only a day.

"Didn't he just go to school?" asked Aglaia.

"Indeed he did not," said Gorgo, the nurse, "and if he was my lad he'd get a licking."

"But, Gorgo, I don't need a licking," exclaimed Theras. "I'll never run away again. Never, never, never!"

Little Opis in her baby way seemed to realise that she had almost lost her big brother. She clung to his hand with her chubby fingers and sat close by him, and if he got up she trotted at his side.

It was soon time to go to bed. Indeed it was past time long ago.

But when they tried to take Opis away, she cried so pitifully that even old Gorgo was sorry.

"There—there, Chicken," she said. "Opis shall sleep to-night right by her big, naughty brother."

"Not naughty—not naughty," said Opis loyally.

Theras was asleep as soon as his curly head touched the pillow, and little Opis lay beside him. Even in her sleep she kept his fingers clasped in her little fist.

CHAPTER XXI

The Splendid Soldier

More than a year had passed when one day there was great excitement in Pheidon's home, even greater than when Theras ran away. For now Pheidon was going on a dangerous journey. He was going to fight for Athens.

Athens had a great many little states which obeyed her. They were small islands lying each by itself in the sea. We would perhaps not think them important because they were so small. But each island had a city of its own, gods of its own, laws of its own making, and money with the picture of its own god or goddess upon it. In each island people had lived for many hundred years. Some of the islands were famous long before Athens was known.

Now one island named Samos had disobeyed Athens and the Athenians were going out to punish it. Perhaps they might have been kinder to little Samos. But the quarrel was on now and good Athenians had to go.

Everybody in the house gathered around Pheidon, trying to do something for him. Most of the slaves were in tears.

There in the aula, Arethusa, with the help of Lampon, was buckling Pheidon's armour to protect him against the spears and swords of the enemy.

First she put on his cuirass, a shining corselet of bronze, covering his chest and back; then the short skirt like a kilt, made of strips of leather covered with metal; then the greaves, or metal leggings, and finally sandals on his feet.

She gave him his shield which a slave had polished so bright that it shone like a mirror. When Theras came near he could see his own face in it, all round like a moon, and the whole aula room like a little reflected picture. In the very middle of the shield was a big letter "A" for Athens.

Then Arethusa reached up and put upon her husband's head the helmet. This, too, was golden-bright and had a red horsehair crest waving softly on top.

At this Theras burst into a shout.

"Oh, Father, what a splendid, splendid soldier!

I did not know you were so beautiful. Oh, Father, let me be a soldier."

"All in good time, my son," said Pheidon solemnly. "You will certainly be a soldier some day."

And now Arethusa threw both arms about her husband's neck and kissed him, then ran away quickly upstairs, lest he should see her weeping. She was not to go down to the ship. That would not have been proper for an Athenian lady.

But Theras was going to the ship. Therefore he was very happy. All the way as they walked together Theras kept looking up at his father, watching how gracefully the tall plume waved in the breeze, how the tip of his lance caught the light. And how strange it sounded, to be sure, to hear him walking, the *click, click* of the leather-metal skirt, the grind and ring of his shield as it struck against the greave.

From every street and corner as they walked along came other Athenian soldiers with their helms, shields, and lances, more and more of them until they were a crowd. Now they all came together to the road between the Long Walls, leading to the harbour.

How splendid they looked! A forest of twinkling lances was moving along together, the helmet crests, red, blue, and orange, were brighter than a garden of flowers. Everybody was talking and laughing.

CHAPTER XXII

THE SLAVE MARKET

Now the road suddenly widened. They were in the harbour town of Piræus. The streets were full of people, for everybody had come to see the soldiers go away in the ships.

"The boy will be suffocated," said Pheidon. "Lampon, lift him up."

So Lampon lifted Theras to his shoulder. Now he could smell the salt water and see, beyond the crowded people, the masts of the ships. He could see the leathern sails, red-orange in colour.

Such a noise! The Agora in Athens was a quiet room compared to this. Here was a sailor quarrelling about his pay, here a lot of shipmasters drunk, having a rousing time. Here a merchant shouted, "Make way for my horses and colts. They're just off the ship." Here a man was mending his boat. *Rap, rap, rap,* sounded his hammer. Slaves were putting heavy loads on the donkeys and urging them along with loud cries.

Now Pheidon led the way through the slave market. A merchant stopped his path.

"Come see my slaves, sir, just landed. Strong workers. Nice gentle house slaves—come look at them."

"Get out of my path," said Pheidon angrily. "Cannot you see that I am going to my ship?"

But just then Theras cried out:

THE SLAVE MARKET

"Father, Father, look over there at the little boy standing on that high block. He's fastened with a chain."

"Yes, son," said Pheidon. "The man is selling him."

"But, Father, he isn't a slave. Look at him."

Pheidon stopped.

"He does not seem like a slave, surely," he said.

The boy was about two years younger than Theras. He was standing very straight with his head up, as if he did not want anybody to think he was a slave. But if you looked at his lips you saw that they were trembling, and his eyes had a far-away look, as if he were hungry for home. Perhaps it was this which made Theras so sorry for him.

"Suppose I had been like that," said Theras with a choke in his voice. "Suppose that toy-man had got me."

"Praise be to Athena!" said Pheidon.

At this moment a hawk-eyed Egyptian stepped up to the block to ask the price of the boy.

At this Theras fairly cried out with terror.

He scrambled down from Lampon's arms before Lampon could catch him, and ran to the block, shouting at the Egyptian:

"You can't have that boy. He's mine, mine, I tell you. My father is buying him for me."

Pheidon quickly followed.

"My child—my dear, headlong boy," he said, "I did not come out with money to buy a slave."

"Oh, but you won't let him be sold!" exclaimed Theras.

He looked so amazed and horrified that Pheidon suddenly changed his mind. He was glad for Theras to be kind.

"My child," he said to the slave boy, "where is your home?"

The slave boy did not answer. I suppose he could not believe that anyone would ever speak kindly to him again. Pheidon had to question him twice over.

Then he seemed to come out of a dream.

"Miletus," he answered.

"And your father was a slave in Miletus, I suppose?" said Pheidon.

"Oh, no, no, no. How can you think my father was a slave!"

Tears brimmed over in the slave boy's eyes. "My father was a great man. That is why the Persian king killed him."

"Oh, ho," said Pheidon seriously. "An enemy of the Great King, was he? Good."

"Yes," answered the boy dreamily. "I will not bow my knee to the Great King."

He was evidently saying something he had heard his father say. And he spoke a pure Ionian Greek.

"By Zeus," said Pheidon angrily, "I won't have true Greeks sold in Athens!"

"Look here, boy. I'm going to pay the price for you, but you are not to be my slave, but my boy's playmate, and as soon as I get home I'll set you free."

The boy with a cry stretched out both his hands to Pheidon, and Pheidon took him in his arms.

Theras reached up and tried to break the chain

which held the boy. But the slave-dealer did that. Then Theras clapped his hands.

"You're going to be my little brother, my brother!" he sang to the boy. But the boy was so astonished that he could only cling to Pheidon and look trembling down at Theras capering about for joy.

CHAPTER XXIII

THE FATHER'S GOING

"WE must make haste," said Pheidon. "I'll be late to my ship. Here, Lampon, take this new boy. I'll take Theras."

Just at this moment Epikides came by dressed in full armour to go.

"Why, Pheidon!" he laughed. "Buying a slave at such a time as this!"

"It was a deed of kindness," said Pheidon. "I want to leave that for my son to remember."

Theras wondered what his father meant by this.

They had been walking fast and now were at the naval harbour, Cantharus. Truly the sea looked as if it were inhabited by gods and dragons. Every ship had some tall painted image at its prow. The ship called the *Boar* had a fierce-looking boar with tusks; the *Nilus* had a crocodile; the *Centaur*, a creature half man, half horse. They were all dancing and moving restlessly on the water, as if they were alive.

Now one ship would sweep up to its dock to take the warriors on board, now another was just starting, or a third was well out in the harbour awaiting the others. Many of these were not warships but large sailing vessels to carry the soldiers. The sails, red and orange, blue and yellow, were bright as a garden of flowers.

Everybody was talking, laughing, shouting orders, and calling good-byes.

Ships are perhaps the most beautiful things which man can make, and among them the sailing ships and triremes are the prettiest. Sail-boats you have seen often, but triremes and biremes are not made these days.

A trireme was a long narrow boat—some were a hundred feet long and more. Far down in the hold near the water-line, on seats either side, sat fifty-four men with oars which stuck through the portholes along the sides of the ship. Above these sat fifty-eight more men with longer oars which stuck through above the others. Above these sat sixty-two oarsmen with still longer oars. Imagine a ship with eighty-seven long oars sweeping along it on either side!

At the bow sat two oar commanders. When these gave the command the oarsmen made ready. Then they called, "Go!" and the three banks of oars, one hundred and seventy-four in all, came down and smote the water with a mighty sound. The water frothed like soapsuds as the boat leaped forward. Only Theras did not think of soapsuds, for he had never seen soap.

"Look, Maro!" he cried, for by now the little boy had told Theras his name. "There comes father's ship now, the *Euterpe*—the one with the goddess at the prow and all the blue pennons flying. Oh, she is coming to the dock!"

Maro dropped Lampon's hand and quickly came to Theras. Like a true little brother he felt that when he held Theras's hand he was happier and safer.

Now like a graceful swan the great trireme *Euterpe* swung into dock — moving, turning, and backing deftly, because it was all human hands that moved her.

The warriors began to march on board. They were all brothers and cousins and relations together. For the Athenians went to war by phatries, or tribes, and that just means families who were related.

Now there was an added stir in the crowd.

"Pericles is coming. Hail, Pericles, Pericles!"

A tall man came swiftly toward the boat. He was the general. He wore helmet and crest and looked indeed like the fine commander he was. He waved to the people and smiled back at their greeting, but he seemed to have too much to think about to talk to anyone.

As Theras was gazing at him, Pheidon hastily bent down and kissed Theras.

"Good-bye, son," he said. "Father is going now. You must be a man and take care of Mother while I am gone."

Theras forgot all the ships and the pretty sights in a moment.

"Father," he cried, "will you come back soon?"

"Yes—yes," answered Pheidon, unclasping Theras's tight hands from his neck.

Theras did not mean to cry, but tears kept coming into his eyes and running over, so he could not help it.

"Look at the warriors going on board," said Lampon. But Theras could not see the warriors. He had not guessed how it would be for Father to go away, and now he did not know what to do.

On the little altar on the deck of the vessel they burned incense to the gods. Now the flute player struck up a tune, the oar master gave command, and, all in time to the pretty tune, down flew the oars. The vessel leaped forward like an agile hound, the sea turned white with foam. Away she leaped—away over the blue water.

Now up went the sails, rippling, snapping, and flapping, now growing steady and smooth as the wind filled them. They were purple sails because Pericles, the general, was on board.

Theras watched it all. But at sight of the vessel, now so small and carrying his dear father off to where the sea met the sky, Theras's heart seemed to break. He sobbed and cried and hid his face.

CHAPTER XXIV

THE RIGHT DOOR

"COME, come," said Lampon, "you mustn't cry like that. What—you with a new little brother all your own? We'll go home now and show him to Mother."

So they hurried through the crowd, back along the road between the Long Walls, and into the city. The sun was setting now, and all along their way they could see the tawny rock of the Akropolis turned pure gold in the light and Athena's spear tipped with fire.

Theras pointed this out to Maro and soon became interested telling him about his new home.

"Let's make him guess which door is ours," said Theras to Lampon.

"I don't see how he can do that," smiled Lampon.

"What does your mother look like?" questioned Maro in a whisper.

"Mother?" answered Theras, laughing. "Oh, she's just Mother."

But Lampon smiled kindly down at the little stranger and said:

"She'll be good to you, little lad, never fear."

They were passing along by the low house doors, each with its guarding Apollo. Suddenly Theras's lips parted and his eyes began to sparkle.

Maro, who was looking at Theras's face, stopped and said:

"This is the door."

And he guessed right.

Just then in the twilight an owl flew on silent wings right past the door and was lost among the housetops.

"Good luck!" cried Lampon. "Our master will come home again. Athena has sent her owl to tell us."

CHAPTER XXV

A Dark Day

For the next few weeks Theras was too busy playing with Maro to think of much else. He must show Maro all the hiding-places in the house, teach him the games the boys played in the street, take him to school, and fight the boys who tried to tease him. It was a splendid thing to have a new little brother. Theras was so busy that he did not notice how pale his mother often was, nor how little she ate at meals. But Maro noticed this.

In these days it was Maro who was Arethusa's chief comfort. When she was sitting lonely in her room Maro would come and sit beside her and lay his head on her knee. She felt that Maro was a real gift of her husband.

One day a cousin of Pheidon's named Metion came to see them. He was Pheidon's nearest of kin. He came to say that the merchant ship in which Pheidon had a great part of his fortune had been sunk by the Samians.

A DARK DAY

"What sad news this will be to tell my dear husband when he comes home," thought Arethusa.

Later Lampon had to tell her that the crops on their farm had failed for the year. This was serious indeed. Theras found his mother in the corner of the room with her hands clasped together and her eyes bright with tears.

"Mother, I'll help; yes, I will," said Theras. "I'll go down to the farm as Father did and see that the slaves work well."

"It is too late now, dear child," said his mother. "The drought has spoiled everything. I must sell some of the farm slaves. That will keep us until Father gets back."

Then one morning came the cousin, Metion, again. At his news the house rang with cries. Metion told them that Pheidon had been killed in the war.

The Samians had taken prisoner a number of Athenian men, and as these were fighting beneath the walls of Samos City the Athenians in the ships had seen Pheidon fall.

What a strange dark morning it was! Theras stood beside his mother, holding her hand. He did not cry, for he couldn't believe that his father would not come back. He felt as if something had struck him out of the dark and was going to strike him again. He was more scared than grieved.

But he stood very straight, remembering how his father had told him to take care of his mother. Aglaia stood on Arethusa's other side with arms about her neck and Opis sat on her lap.

Poor Arethusa! There was nothing for an Athenian lady to do but sit at home. She would not be allowed to work and support her children. She must depend upon some kinsman to help.

About a week later Cousin Metion came in again.

CHAPTER XXVI

A Darker Day

ARETHUSA hated to see Metion come. And well she might. He was a selfish man who had stayed at home to save his own goods. He was half angry with Pheidon for getting killed, and very angry that all Pheidon's fortune had been lost.

He had with him a man strange to Arethusa—an old man with shrewd grey eyes who kept looking at Theras as if he saw no one else in the room.

"This is my mother's cousin, Hippias," said Metion. "He comes from Sparta."

Arethusa rose to greet them with Opis in her arms. She remembered this unusual relationship with the rival city. She had somehow felt that it made Metion even more disagreeable than he otherwise would have been.

"He's going to help," continued Metion. "You see, I've got to take you and your daughters into my house. I'll close this house and sell it. That will help me to support you. But Hippias will take the boy."

"Hippias take what boy?" asked Arethusa, very white.

"Your son, Theras, of course."

"Oh, I have to take care of Mother," said Theras. "Father said so."

"You were not asked to speak," said Hippias, frowning.

"Pheidon's son cannot go to Sparta," said Arethusa firmly. "Pheidon could not bear that."

"He doesn't have to bear it," said Metion. "He's dead."

"Sparta!" cried out Theras. "Oh, I cannot go there. I could not live anywhere but in Athens."

"You'll live in Sparta and learn not to speak before your elders," said Hippias.

Then he told Arethusa not unkindly how he had lost both his sons in battle and was most thankful to find a child of Metion's kindred to adopt as his son. He had a large fortune and when he died the fortune would belong to Theras.

Arethusa saw that there was no way out of it. She would not be allowed to work and support Theras herself and she must not take away from him the fortune which Hippias would give him.

"Then let me say good-bye to my son," she said.

Hippias had told her he was leaving Athens that morning.

She took Theras to her own room. There she put her arms around him and told him to remember never, never to become a Spartan.

"Oh, Mother, how could I be a Spartan?" cried Theras. "I'm an Athenian."

"Never believe what they teach you about Athens."

"No, no," he answered, clinging to her.

"And as soon as you are big enough, come back to Mother."

"Oh, Mother, I'll come back. I won't live in Sparta, I won't."

"You will soon be big. The Spartan ways will make you strong. Then you will come back. Goodbye, dear—dearest child. You must be a man to-day. Remember you are an Athenian. You are coming back to Athens."

She was so quiet and serious that Theras stopped crying and held up his head.

All the slaves came into the aula to say good-bye to Theras, but Arethusa would not let them, for fear they would make him cry again. She made them all go away, even Lampon.

Hippias was ready now and waiting by the front door. Arethusa got out Theras's clothes and wrapped a little bundle for Hippias's slave to carry. Little Aglaia and Opis kissed him without knowing why, and Maro kissed him and ran quickly away.

Then Arethusa led him to the front door. There she knelt down and took him once more close in her arms.

"Remember," she whispered.

And Theras could not answer, though he knew he would remember always.

PART II.—SPARTA

PART II.—SPARTA

CHAPTER XXVII

THE OLD MAN HIPPIAS

SURELY never was there a sadder little boy than Theras as he walked away through the streets of his beloved town that late summer morning.

The narrow streets of the Kerameikos looked very dear to him. Each door with its stiff little Apollo standing guard beside it was a well-known door to Theras. He knew the boys who lived in the houses. Would he ever see them again? And the boys at school, Telamon, Koretas, Klinias. Theras was glad that none of them were on the streets at this early hour. He would have hated to hear Klinias ask, "Where are you going?" or hear Koretas say, "Theras, who is that rough old man holding your hand?"

For all the way his foster-father kept tight hold of Theras's hand, and a slave walked on the other side of Theras.

All of a sudden one of the doors opened and out came old Lysander, one of the judges of Athens, a friend of Pheidon's. With him were several men. They were all talking.

Quickly Theras pulled his hand free of Hippias and ran towards his father's friend.

"Lysander, oh, Lysander," he called. "Save me! They are taking me away. Oh, o—oh!" he screamed.

For someone snatched at his shoulders and the slave was dragging him back to Hippias, who promptly boxed him on both ears.

"You young fox," said he, "how dare you scream out like that?"

Now Theras had never been struck before. He was so indignant that Hippias should hit him out here in the open street that without thinking at all Theras doubled up his fists and fell to pummelling the old gentleman's chest like a drum.

Hippias was so surprised that he almost tumbled backward.

"You," cried Theras, "you shall not hit me—you, you coward!"

But the slave seized Theras again and hustled him along as fast as he could, while Hippias pulled himself together and followed.

Now if Lysander had really heard Theras there is hardly a doubt that he would have saved him from leaving Athens, and Theras would have been spared many a hardship and sorrowful day.

But Lysander did not hear. He was old and a little deaf. He thought it was all just a street fight, which was common enough in Athens.

CHAPTER XXVIII

THE LAST SIGHT OF ATHENS

AT the Dipylon Gate were a number of Spartans awaiting Hippias.

"Hail, Hippias," they called.

"Why, Hippias," said one, "you look ruffled. What has happened to you?"

"Just a bit of Athenian manners," answered Hippias with a kind of laugh which somehow was not a laugh.

"Athenian manners!" repeated the Spartan. "By Zeus, the Athenians are barbarians."

"They call themselves good fighters," scoffed another. "They don't stop talking long enough to fight."

"Humph," grunted the cousin. "I don't know about that," and he rubbed his chest.

Theras was so angry to hear them scoffing at Athens that he forgot the sorrow of passing for ever out of Athens's gate.

The party now walked swiftly along the country road. Theras had much ado to keep up with them. Presently they came to the stream Kiphissos. There was no bridge across it. There were but few bridges anywhere in Greece.

The Spartans had to wade across the stream. But before they did so they all said a little prayer asking the stream to let them go across, because they believed a god or goddess dwelt in the stream. That was what made it alive and made it run and murmur.

But Theras made a prayer all his own.

"O Kiphissos, god of this stream," he begged. "bring me back! Bring me back to Athens. If you will bring me back I will give you a gift. Wine and barley will I pour into your stream. I don't know where I shall get it, but I will surely, surely give you a gift. O Kiphissos, remember to bring me back!"

Then the men hurried forward again. They soon began to mount the hill Aigaleos. How often Theras had come here with the boys and their pedagogues. At the very top the hill-road suddenly came out from between high banks on the bare crest.

Theras could see from here in every direction. Before him the road ran down to the shore of a lovely little bay—the Bay of Salamis—where once the Greek ships had met the Persian ships and beaten them in battle. All Greeks were proud of this because the Persians had had four times as many ships. Yet the Greeks had beaten them.

"Look, Salamis," said the Spartans proudly, for they also had had part in that battle.

But Theras did not look at the Bay of Salamis. He looked back at Athens. For he knew that this was the last sight he would get of the city. Certainly he would never see Athens again unless he made a great fight to get back, and Theras did not know even how to begin that fight.

The sun had risen over Hymettos Mountain. In the flooding morning light lay the little city. Theras could see the splendid wall that went about it, within which Athens was so safe. He could see the open square of the Agora, or market, and the Kerameikos district where his own home stood. He could see the trees of the Lyceum Gymnasium where he was to have gone as soon as he was old enough. Boys less high-born had to go to the Kynosarges Gymnasium outside the wall. But Theras was to have gone to the best.

Most of all he could see the Akropolis full in the morning sunlight, and all the dear temples shining and glittering. No city in all Greece had temples like these. He could even catch a glimpse of the great bronze Athena with her hand upraised as if to beckon him back. She seemed to be saying, "Come back home, Theras. Why are you going away?"

Suddenly Hippias shook Theras roughly.

"Stop staring at that good-for-nothing burg," he said crossly. "We can't wait all day."

If Theras had had any voice at all he would have answered Hippias back, and perhaps have got a whipping. But he was too choked with tears to speak.

As he followed his foster-father down the farther hill Theras thought:

"Never mind, you old Hippias. It would take many more words than you can ever say to make me believe that my dear, dear Athens is not the best city in all the world."

CHAPTER XXIX

Rivals in the Games

The Spartans strode along the road in silence. Athenian men would have talked all the while about what they were passing, about the wars and politics of their own city, about wonderful plays and stories—anything! And that would have made the way seem short. But the Spartans, young or old, said nothing.

They passed without a word the little town of Eleusis. Here the same slave who had caught Theras in the street, and whose name was Hermos, came up, and, since they were behind the others, began to jeer at Theras.

"Hi, hit the master, did ye? I wouldn't take the whipping you'll get. Oh, not for a hundred drachmas."

Theras turned upon him.

"Do Hippias's slaves speak impudence to his son?" he asked loudly.

He thought the slave would answer him again. But, big man though he was, Hermos shrank away scared to death. Hippias must be very harsh with his slaves to make them so fearful as that.

It was after nightfall that they reached Megara. Here they found an inn—a miserable, dark hovel where the beds were foul and hard as boards.

But Theras was so tired that he slept all night as if with one long, deep breath.

Agis, one of the younger Spartans, shook him

awake. Theras could hardly drag himself from the bed. It was very early, before sunrise.

Theras had heard much of Megara. It was the town nearest to Athens and a great rival. At least it had once been a rival, but Athens had long ago gone ahead of Megara in everything.

Theras, as he passed through the streets, looked contemptuously at the small temples. He remembered, too, how much better the Athenian boys had showed themselves in the Olympian Games last year. They had taken the prizes from the Megarians every time —in the long jump, in running races, and in that fivefold prize called the pentathlon.

Theras would have liked to call out: "Hey, you Megarians, who won the prize at Olympia!"

CHAPTER XXX

THE ROBBERS' ROCKS

BUT soon Megara was far behind. Theras and the Spartans were swinging along the country road again. The Spartans seemed never to tire. But they were grown men. Agis, the youngest, was eighteen. And Theras was only a boy.

Presently the way became rougher and rougher. They were in the mountains, and the road was a mere track among the stones. They climbed up and up, and yet the mountain peaks soared above them to the sky. As far as Theras could see were mountains, and not a house in sight. But on the left of the road far down below them were steep cliffs and the sea. The sun was setting and all the sea was as red as wine.

"I suppose we'd better stop here," grunted Hippias. "We've come to the Skironian Rocks. That's a good place to spend the night."

The others laughed as if this were a huge joke. And Theras knew why they laughed.

The Skironian Rocks had always been a hiding-place for robbers. Travellers again and again would be waylaid here, beaten, perhaps killed, and their goods and valuables taken. The Spartans being a company of armed men thought they could manage any robbers.

In the very oldest time these rocks had been the home of a robber named Skiron. Skiron had a convenient way of throwing people over the cliff to be devoured by a huge tortoise that lived down there by the sea's edge. Another robber thereabout had a bed upon which he would lay his victim. If you were too long, Procrustes (that was his name) would cut off your legs; if too short, he would pull your legs out. Very funny this seemed to Procrustes, but it was hardly funny to anyone else.

Long ago a splendid hero named Theseus had come this way, had killed both Procrustes and Skiron, and had thrown Skiron down to his own pet tortoise to be eaten.

His father, Pheidon, had many times told Theras the story of Theseus, and now he looked about the savage place, almost expecting Theseus to appear again.

The Spartans sat down, opened up some bundles, and ate their supper of bread and cheese. Athenians at a time like this would certainly have had out a lyre. Somebody would have played and sung to make merry. But the Spartans ate in silence. Instead of keeping Theras with them, they gave him his supper to eat on a rock by himself some distance away.

He was very lonely and so tired with the two long days' walk that his back and legs ached. He ate his supper hungrily and wished for more, but did not dare to ask. Then he stretched himself wearily on the rocks, looking down the road by which they had come.

All day long Theras had watched every turn of the road, hoping he could remember the way. Some day he might be coming back alone. Indeed, he must know the road. How far away seemed Athens now! Oh, in another world, so different from this lonely world of rock and sea. In Athens at this hour, Lampon would be lighting the torch in the aula. Mother would be sitting there with the baby Opis in her arms. She always sang. Theras could almost hear the song:

> Vesperus sinks in the glorying west;
> Sleep, little Opis, and take thy rest.
> Swallows circle down from the sky,
> Circling twittering, bye, oh, bye.
> Sleep, little Opis, lullaby.

Oh, Theras heard it now quite clear and plain. Why was it he could not creep up behind Mother and throw his arms about her? Why could he not touch her? Why? Because he was sound asleep!

CHAPTER XXXI

Surprise by Night

ABOUT midnight Theras awoke because he was so cold. He had curled himself up like a dog or cat, but he was still shivering. The Spartans on their higher slope were all lying asleep around the embers of a fire. Even the young man who was sitting up to watch had his head bowed upon his breast.

"I don't believe he's watching," thought Theras. "He looks sound asleep."

The old story of Skiron came back to memory. Of course Skiron was dead, but this was still a great place for robbers.

A wicked place it looked in the starlight, with jutting rocks and clefts where men could hide. Just above the road was a forest of fir trees, black and still. There was no wind, but the sea beating restlessly far below was loud in the stillness.

"If Aglaia were here," thought Theras, "wouldn't she be scared! Of course, she's a girl. But a boy like me——"

Then his heart stood still.

A twig had cracked in the forest just as though someone had stepped on it. No, now he heard only the sea, *wash—wash—wash*-ing on the beach. Theras wished the sea would keep still so he could listen. It might have been a fox or a bear he had heard.

Theras decided that it was nothing at all.

Then *crack, crack*, came the sound again—cautious—surely a step! But if Theras should waken the Spartans they'd laugh at him. They'd call him a coward. An Athenian coward!

Something, he knew not what, drew Theras's eyes in another direction.

There, creeping out from behind a rock into the road, were two men. He saw them plainly.

With a yell, Theras leaped to his feet and toward the Spartans.

"Robbers, robbers!" he cried. "They're in the woods! They're down the road!"

The Spartans sprang up quick as cats, each right hand to its sword.

"Little fool!" snapped the sentinel. "I'd have seen them. I was——"

"Silence!" commanded Hippias. "Listen, will you!"

And just as he spoke a stone dislodged in the forest came clattering down. Then a stone missile hit the sentinel full in the chest.

"To the forest. Quick!" rang out Hippias's voice.

And like one man the band of Spartans leaped and clambered up into the woods. If the robbers were to have the protection of trees, the Spartans would have it too.

Hippias, old as he was, seemed able to keep up with the others. He caught Theras's hand, but Theras jerked it away as they were running and scrambling.

"A sword," gasped Theras. "If only I had a sword!"

Hippias snatched from his own belt a dagger and

handed it to the boy. Theras felt now that he could fight for himself, even though he was only a boy.

Now all were in the forest. Suddenly in the darkness one of the Spartans bumped full into a robber, and instantly they were grappling. Nobody could see in the black shadow and confusion. But a cry rang out and oaths in a wild, barbarous dialect. Then Agis's voice shouting:

"Ho, ho, I've got him! I've got him!"

There was another cry, a stabbing blow. Then silence. The Spartan's short sword had thrust home.

And with that the robbers stampeded up the hill, crashing through boughs, stumbling over rocks—away, away!

CHAPTER XXXII

On Guard now

THE Spartans followed. But only for a few moments. It was useless to try to find the robbers in that wilderness of rocks and trees. Also the robbers might circle around and even yet get to the Spartan camp.

So Hippias and the rest returned to guard their goods. You may be sure they kept alert now. They retraced their steps down the road to a better position —a little hill which Hippias remembered. They made the slaves carry all the goods and burdens back to the top of this hillock, free on all sides, so that they could see in every direction as far as the starlight would let them see, but with crags behind which they could hide. They built no fire to tell the robbers where they were, but stood wrapped in their cloaks, watching. This time Theras stood with them.

He forgot to be tired. He forgot even to wish for Athens. He seemed to be acting in some wonderful story like Theseus himself or Odysseus, who met with so many adventures by sea and land.

So the hours passed.

Suddenly old Hippias spoke up in anger.

"Skyllis," said he to the young man who had been sentinel, "how is it that you let those villainous thieves creep up to our very elbows? Why didn't you call out long before?"

Skyllis began to make excuse.

"Oh, sir, I did call out. I——"

"You did not. It was the youngster here, Theras, who awoke us, not you. You were asleep. I'll have you punished when we get to Sparta, you lying good-for-naught."

"But, Hippias, hear me!"

"Be quiet," said Hippias rudely. "Look here, Theras. You anyhow were watching. Wasn't Skyllis asleep?"

Now Theras had been taught by Pheidon never to be a tale-bearer. "Everybody," so Pheidon had told him, "everybody hates the teller of evil stories. Even those who want to hear the story hate him who tells."

So Theras answered quickly:

"I do not know, Hippias. I was watching the forest where I heard the noise. I only know Skyllis was sitting straight up."

"Straight up, hey? Are you sure?"

"Yes, I am sure."

"Humph," grunted the old man, peering at Theras again. "Humph."

Then silence fell once more.

And so they stood until the grey light showed them the road at the foot of the hill, and the sea far below —a silver mist.

Then dawn arose with unspeakable splendour out of the sea.

Theras watched the moving rosy clouds, the open rifts where he could see into the very deeps of the golden sky. Once he was almost certain that there above the sea he glimpsed a slender goddess shouldering her way through the skyey spaces and the mists.

But she was swiftly gone, and immediately the sun was too bright even for his young eyes.

"Could I really have seen her," he wondered— "Aurora at her daily task of lighting up the east?"

"Here, boy." Hippias shook his shoulder. "Don't stand there staring like an idiot. Don't you see we're starting?"

CHAPTER XXXIII

THE SPARTAN WAY

SURE enough, the others were running down the hill and were far along the road. Joyously Theras ran after them. Soon he came to the place of last night's battle. Then he saw Agis, the young man who had killed the robber, come running out of the forest. He was dragging something. Great Zeus! Agis was dragging the bloodstained body of his antagonist down the hill and shouting as he came. On he pranced, dragging the poor, pitiful thing across the road to the cliff's edge, where with a kick he sent it flying down, down into the sea.

"There you go," he yelled savagely. "May the old tortoise eat you. May the gods forget you, you and all your children."

The other Spartans shouted in cruel glee. But Theras suddenly hid his eyes, shivering as if with cold.

He could not eat his breakfast that morning though Hippias urged him.

"You're a fool," he said, "not to eat when you have a whole day's journey ahead. What ails you, anyway?"

All morning Theras walked the rocky road in a dull, cold horror. Over and over again he could see the poor robber's body bouncing down over the stones, then flinging over the edge into the golden sea. Dead people who were never buried became ghosts who wandered for ever trying to find rest.

So the Athenian people believed and so did his old nurse, Gorgo, who, full of superstitions, had told him. Now the poor robber could never, never rest day after day, night after night. For this reason the Greek considered it a great sin not to bury a dead man.

Presently Agis himself, who had done this thing, came back and began to walk beside Theras. Theras turned away his face so as not to look at him.

"By Hermes, what's the matter with you?" asked Agis. "You have done nothing but sulk the whole time. Most boys would think themselves lucky going to Sparta as the heir of Hippias."

Lucky! It was just what Theras considered the worst luck of his life.

"I wouldn't want to go to Sparta as the heir of both your kings," he said flatly. "My city is Athens."

Of course, this was quite impolite of Theras. But Agis had not been polite to the robber.

"Humph," grunted Agis, for all the world like Hippias himself. "That's all very well for you to say, Theras. But Athens wasn't treating you so well that I could see. You'd lost your father, your money—everything. Athenian orphans have a pretty rough time getting along. You must have heard that, my boy."

Theras's cheeks flushed angrily.

"I'd rather be poor in Athens than rich anywhere else," he retorted. "At least I'd be in *Athens* and trying to do what my father told me to do."

"And what was that?"

"Take care of my mother and sisters. Oh, I know

A SHIP ON LAND

some of Father's friends would help me. They'd know I was growing up and would pay them back."

"You pay them back," mocked Agis. "I never before saw a chicken just out of its shell that kept crowing like a full-grown cock."

"I'd do more than crow if I were there in Athens," insisted Theras. But his voice broke a little as he remembered how often he had neglected to help his mother when he could. Here on the Spartan road Theras felt suddenly grown up, as if he could really take his father's place.

But Agis only looked at him with scorn.

"What a fool ye be," he said, and walked away.

CHAPTER XXXIV

A Ship on Land

THE next night stop of the little party was Corinth. But before they reached there they came to the famous Isthmus of Corinth. This is a narrow neck of land, in some places only two miles wide, which separates the two seas. Corinth was called the City of the Two Seas because it was on both the Gulf of Corinth and the Ægean Sea. And the ships of Corinth were the most famous of all Greece.

There was a track of wood laid straight across the Isthmus from water to water, and upon this the Corinthians could drag their ships from the Gulf to the Ægean Sea. It saved them hundreds of miles sailing around the peninsula of Greece.

As Theras came near the trackway he could hear men singing in chorus, and the awful creaking and squeaking and groaning of the ship. The men were singing one song over and over again:

>Yo, heave ho!
>Come fast, come slow,
>Come to the sea, you ship!
>The lazy land,
>The mud, the sand,
>The land's no place for a ship!
>Yo, heave ho!
>Come fast, come slow,
>Come to the sea, you ship!

Theras ran ahead of the Spartans, and there soon he saw the whole thing—the great slow hulk of the vessel, with a dragon-head at the prow, rearing high and grinning at the men.

It seemed to answer, "I won't come," but come it did, every time the men gave a long, steady pull at the ropes.

At the slanting beach the ship slid faster. The men splashed ahead of it into the water—laughing, singing, pulling. Then with a shout, "Look alive!" they leaped aside, and—*zoom, zipp, splash*—the ship went into the deep tide, skimming away with sudden ease, like a bird set free. It left the wooden ways smoking from its swift descent.

Theras clapped his hands with delight.

"Well, well," said his foster-father, watching him from under bushy brows, "ye liked that, did ye?"

"Yes, yes. Look how far the ship is already. I can see the helmsman guiding it."

Later in the afternoon they came to the Isthmian Stadion. Here was a place of athletic games almost as famous as Olympia itself. Many a young Athenian had won the prize there for leaping, running, or disc-throwing. Pheidon had always told Theras that if he would practise running he might soon run at the Isthmian Games. Then after that at Olympia itself.

Theras climbed up the empty seats tier after tier to the very top. The stadion was in a hollow of the hillside, wind-swept, and sweet with the smell of the sea. From the top Theras looked down into the running place where weeds and flowers and thyme were growing. For it had been a number of months since the games had been held.

How would it feel to be running down there when these seats were full of people looking down upon him—swaying with excitement, cheering, laughing, some cheering Theras on, some cheering the other fellow if the other fellow happened to be ahead? Great Hermes, he would almost die if he did not win. Father had been a good runner. Theras would practise and—— He looked up. Hippias was beside him, panting from the climb.

"Oh, Hippias, may I come here next year and enter the games if I practise my running? I am a pretty good runner. Father said so."

"Yes, I think so. D'ye think ye could run well enough to be an honour to Sparta and to me?"

To Sparta! The words were like a dagger thrust into Theras. That he should run for Sparta and not for dear Athens!

He put his head down and walked silently away.

CHAPTER XXXV

Sparta is so Different from Athens

THERAS was still dreaming of this when he ran plump into Agis. Theras turned quickly from him, but Agis roughly caught his elbow.

"Look here, you young sour-face! For what do you look at me like that—as if I were poison!"

Theras opened his mouth but shut it again. He did not want to answer.

"Out with it," said Agis. "I've had just enough of your glumness."

"I hate what you did to that robber," said Theras heartily. "You had no right to throw his poor body into the sea."

"No right, hey?" laughed Agis. He stood there with hands on hips, looking down at Theras, teasing—a handsome figure.

"No," said Theras. "Killing him was enough."

"You seem to forget that I saved you and the whole party by getting him first."

"No, I do not forget that."

"How about your Athenian hero, Theseus? Didn't

AT LAST—SPARTA 95

he kill the robber Skiron and throw him over the cliff? I was imitating him."

Theras did not know what to answer to this. He looked up into Agis's face. Suddenly Theras remembered the whole thing again and his eyes filled with horror and disgust.

"I don't care," he said. "It was mean to do it. And it was sacrilege. Now the poor robber ghost will wander everywhere always."

Agis looked scared, for all Spartans believed in ghosts.

"We Athenians wouldn't have done it," added Theras suddenly. "Killing him was enough."

Unconsciously Theras had explained the whole difference between Athens and Sparta. Athens always knew when to stop, Sparta never did.

As for Agis, he frowned and walked away.

CHAPTER XXXVI

At Last—Sparta!

THE next stop of the little party was Tegea. From here they started before dawn, for the next stop was to be Sparta itself. At last from a low hill they saw the whole city. All the Spartans were as jolly as could be to get home.

Now Theras had not expected Sparta to be much of a city, but he had thought it would be better than this. It was a straggling town. The homes were mean and small, and not only the homes but the temples also—a remarkable thing in Greece. They had no Akropolis for their temples, and most of all they had no wall about Sparta. This to Theras's eyes made it look poor indeed. All the temples were very old—simple things of a bygone day.

Now it had so happened that Athens, a few years ago, had been burned—the whole of it—by the Persians. But the brave thrifty Athenians had built it all new again, ten times more beautiful than it had been, ten times more beautiful indeed than any other city in the world. No wonder that to an Athenian boy Sparta looked poor.

Then to cap all, no blue sea was there—only mountains, mountains, mountains seeming to shut off all the world.

The Spartans trudged down the hill and across the bridge that led over the small stream, Eurotas, and entered the narrow streets of Sparta. Theras walked silently with them, thinking only of home.

Quite unexpectedly they came to a large open space. At the far end was a grove of trees. At one side was a stadion for running. But directly in front of the party was a large, flat drilling ground where a hundred boys were drilling.

They were boys just Theras's age, but they were going through the military drill like grown soldiers. In Athens the boys performed choruses and even soldierly dances, but nothing like this, nothing so skilful.

AT LAST—SPARTA

The Spartan boys were quite naked, and brown as berries. They were thin and swift as birds, yes, and birdlike in their grace and sureness. Theras was to learn later why they were so thin.

Gracious, how quick they were! At the very instant of command they obeyed. Sometimes they leaped forward holding up their targets and ducking beneath them. Sometimes they rushed forward with spears set so as to make an even wall in front of them. Terrible it was to see that deadly wall advance. Then suddenly they stopped, tiptoe, turned altogether, swooped back again, away and away in apparent confusion. But when at the far end of the drill ground they stopped — turned! Behold, every boy was in place and the spears ranged even, as before.

They were like a flock of pigeons when they have a good leader, and so sweep up high in air, then down, circling, dipping, alighting, all in perfect formation.

Theras was so excited that he fairly danced where he stood. He pulled his foster-father's sleeve.

"Hippias," he said, "shall I belong to that company? Let me belong to that company!"

"Hey? Yes, yes. You like it, do you? Of course you shall belong. Hi, Terpander, come hither, will you?" he called.

The young leader halted the company with a sharp command and came respectfully over to Hippias.

"This," said Hippias, "is my new adopted son." He pushed Theras forward. "I want you to 'choose' him into a company."

Terpander tried not to look astounded, bowed

again, then took Theras's hand and to the boy's great embarrassment led him in front of the whole regiment.

"Lochos formation!" he called. And instantly the boys divided off into small groups of from twenty to thirty boys, each with a youth for captain at its head.

"Here's a new member. What company will have him? You are to vote on it. You, Thalates, you first put the vote to your company."

It took Theras some moments to realise what they were doing—actually voting upon him right before his face and, what was worse, turning him down. Theras was aware that Thalates put some question to his company which the company met with angry silence. Then Thalates called "No's?" And the whole little company shouted "No!" with a vim.

The next company tried him. Again the shout of "No!" A third company began.

By this time Theras was hot all over with shame. His throat filled up and his eyes too. Then his eyes cleared.

He turned wrathfully towards Hippias.

"If I had a new son," he cried out, "I wouldn't see him shamed by the whole town. I wouldn't see him sold like a slave at an auction."

Then Theras bolted. He hadn't any plan. He was only going to run away from such rude people.

Someone caught him. It was Agis, laughing, mocking Agis. Agis had a great struggle to hold him. Then he handed Theras over to Thalates.

"Hold hard, Thalates," he laughed. "He's slippery as a satyr."

Then Agis disappeared. Theras was too occupied kicking, struggling, panting, to care what Agis might be doing.

But presently Agis came back.

"Now, young fire-eater," he said, "come along with me. I'm your captain. I'm the only one here who can stand your impudence."

If Theras had stopped to consider he might have guessed that Agis was doing him a friendly turn. However, Theras did not think that, nor have any hope concerning Agis. And it was well, for Agis proved a sharp and stern captain. Nothing friendly about him.

CHAPTER XXXVII

Spartan Boys are Soldiers

Theras was at once put into line, and the drill proceeded. It was ever so much harder than he had supposed. In the first place, the manœuvres were performed with wonderful swiftness. In the second place, the commands were given in the broad Doric dialect which, while it was Greek, was so different from Athenian Greek that Theras could not understand the words.

If we were to go to Scotland and hear the people

there speak English we could not make it out at all. It is broad Scotch and sounds at first like a different language.

So when the boys leaped forward, Theras's leap came far after the others. When they faced about or charged at a run, they overtook him, knocked him down, leaped over him, and skurried onward, yelling:

"Look at girlie, look at Kora."

They called Theras "girlie" because his hair was long. All boys in Athens wore long hair until they grew up to be epheboi, or youths. Then they cut off their hair. Of course, the custom in Sparta was just opposite. Boys were short-haired and on growing up let their hair grow long. All Spartan men had long hair.

Still they called Theras "girlie, girlie." Their word for it was "Kora," but Theras knew well what they meant.

Theras was already hot and exhausted from his long walking journey. But nobody seemed to remember that. As for Theras, he kept on trying until the drill stopped. He made one great resolve. He would learn that drill so as to do it just as well as any Spartan.

At last they were being marched away from the Dromos, or drill ground.

"To Eurotas," was the command.

Tired as he was, Theras was so in earnest about the drill that he forgot to think of home. His only thought was, "I'm going to learn that drill. I'll work till I know it."

At the river bank (the Eurotas) the boys halted.

There were slaves waiting who gave them small sickles, and instantly all the boys fell to work cutting the rushes which grew at the river's edge. Theras could not imagine why they did this. Were they going to make baskets of the rushes? That was slave work, unfit for a freeborn boy. But there was no telling what these curious Spartans might be set to do.

Not one of the boys told him. Not one said, "Cut your rushes. You'll be sorry if you don't."

So Theras stood and watched them, his sickle in his hand.

Then at a command of Thalates they all marched back to the town. They stopped by a low building made of dried mud which was their barracks. Here they laid their rushes on the floor, each boy arranging a pile of them.

"Hi, Kora's got no bed," they jeered.

And then Theras remembered that Spartan boys always slept on rushes, which they must gather for themselves. They had no other beds.

For supper the boys had only some black, hard bread and the worst soup Theras had ever tasted. It seemed to be made of vinegar and salt. He was so hungry that he ate both bread and soup; and from the way the Spartan boys licked their plates (they had horrid table manners) Theras saw that they were hungry, too, even when they had finished.

Then they marched back from the messroom and went to bed. Theras, having no rushes, took the bare floor. But so tired was he that he slept soundly all the night through.

CHAPTER XXXVIII

Getting used to it

The first day in Sparta passed like a real soldier's day—marching, drilling, eating at long tables with the captain at their head. All this was new to Theras and interested him mightily. He liked to be a soldier. The following day when the boys plunged into the Eurotas for their morning bath, they began to race in swimming. Theras dashed after them and beat everyone. For all Athenian boys were fine swimmers. This made the boys respect him. And that day one of the boys, Drako, gave Theras a spear—a great token of friendship.

It was the third day when Theras's lochos, or company, went with the older boys up into the forests of the mountain to hunt boars. The Taÿgetos Mountains were very wild and rugged, much more so than any region round about Athens. There were deep glens where the boys had to cut their way through undergrowth, as if nobody since the world began had ever been there before them. There were steep hillsides where only by holding hands and pulling each other could they clamber up at all.

Now in the heights the hounds began to run about as if they were crazy, holding their noses to the ground, yelping and baying.

"They've caught the scent," cried the boys and ran after the dogs in hot pursuit.

GETTING USED TO IT

How wonderful for Theras to see at last the great beast crashing through the bushes, leaping along so swiftly, though his pig shape looked so clumsy. Then in a hollow the boar turned and fought the dogs. Great Artemis! what tusks he had—how wildly he squealed. What a fierce fighter he was!

Agis, who always seemed in the forefront of everything, leaped forward and speared the boar full in the breast. Others followed and soon the splendid, savage boar was killed.

That evening Theras's company did not go back to the barracks, but were allowed to stay out in the fields. They built a great fire. The slaves busied themselves cutting up the boar, and soon the tenderest parts of the meat were roasting on the fire. Then they feasted on the juicy pork as only hungry boys in the open can feast.

Theras never forgot that night. The sweet dampness of the air, the smell of the pork, the leaping and crackling of the flames conquering the night, and far away the dark forms of the Taÿgetos Mountains lifting among the stars. And with it all the feeling of being grown up—a man.

They slept all night on the ground.

Is it any wonder that Theras, among such adventures, felt happy and amused?

Was he forgetting Athens? Was he becoming a real Spartan? Theras was too occupied to think of this. But it certainly looked as though he were doing so.

All this while something was weighing upon Theras—his foster-father's whipping. Hippias had threatened to whip him, yet he had not done so. No boy was spared or excused in Sparta, and Theras had hit his uncle. Oh, Hippias was sure to whip him for that. It was no happy thing this, to feel a whipping hanging over his head and yet put off from day to day.

One afternoon he met Hippias and stopped in his path.

"Well," spoke the old man, "and how do you like the drill? You did not get on so well that first day, eh?"

"No, but I'm beginning to now," said Theras with brightening face. "This morning I kept with them every turn."

"Yes, so I heard."

"Hippias," began Theras, then stopped.

"Well—out with it!"

"If you're going to whip me, I wish you would do it now. I—I do not like to keep expecting——"

"You do not know how hard I whip," said Hippias.

"Yes, I do. I've seen the other boys get whippings. That's the trouble. Oh, please do it now. The boys say you always whip when you promise a whipping."

"Young man," said Hippias severely, "you must weigh words better. Harmos promised the whipping, and Agis promised it also. *I* never did. But if you *want* it as a favour——" He lifted his hand and Theras dodged away.

"Then you are really not going to whip me?" he cried, delighted. "Athena be praised!"

"Artemis be praised, you'd better say. It's Artemis has to do with whippings."

Hippias laughed harshly. Somehow Theras did not like that laugh. It seemed to mock him. However, he walked back to his barracks quite happy of heart.

CHAPTER XXXIX

HOMESICK

YES, Theras, in spite of himself, was contented in Sparta. The days lengthened into months. He mastered the drill so that he never made a mistake and was as quick as the best of them. He learned the droning chant of Spartan Laws which the boys went through every morning. He learned to understand the curious Doric talk. Then something happened.

Theras never quite knew what it was. But something made him unhappy and restless. Something made him feel more a stranger in Sparta than he had been on the very first day.

Theras had been interested learning Spartan ways. Now he knew them. The newness had worn off.

First of all he began to miss the story-songs which the Athenian boys were so proud to know by heart—the adventures of heroes in far-away places, their journey by land and sea, their brave deeds. When learning or singing such stories Theras had always seemed carried off to the distant lands where these things had happened.

*D

Then at the Athenian school it had been such a pleasant change to hear the master say briskly, "Time's up. Go out now to athletic practice."

In Athens things were always changing.

But now that Theras had learned the Spartan drill, how stupid it was to go through it again and again with no difference. Now that he had learned the chant of laws (a dull song at best), how dreary to go through it every morning, every morning!

In Sparta every day was the same.

Theras asked one of the boys:

"Simmias, when do we begin to have Homer songs?"

"Homer songs!" scoffed Simmias. "Never, Sissy. Play the lyres and sing? That's for hired slaves."

Now Theras knew that Homer was not for hired slaves. In Theras's family it had been a particular pride to know splendid songs and to lead the choruses in Athens. And oh, his father—what splendid story-songs he had sung, what splendid deeds he had told of to his little boy! These Spartan boys hardly saw their fathers. The fathers came sometimes to the barracks to see them, but so distant and severe they were.

"When do you boys go home?" Theras asked.

Again Simmias scoffed at him.

"Home! We don't go home. We are not babies. We are in barracks now."

Yes, they were in barracks. And a very bare and lonely place it was compared to Theras's home with Father, Mother, sisters, and loving slaves.

HOMESICK

Mother! Of course, Theras did not dare to tell any Spartan boy that he thought of his mother. But he did, and that often. How long it seemed since he had seen her! It seemed a year, and he had had no word from her. Mother had promised to send him a message if she ever had a chance. She could not write. No woman could write in those days.

Still Theras kept hoping that he would get a message from her. Yes, from Mother, but not from Father. No matter how long Theras waited, no matter how long Theras lived, he would never have any message from his father. He would never, never see his father's face again.

Only now did the truth of this come down upon Theras. The truth and the sorrow. Theras had always loved his father best of anybody. But now he loved him ten times more.

Now every night Theras would dream of his father or else of someone at home—Mother, Opis, Lampon. And he would awake with a cry. For just as he awakened, the dear one would fade away. Sometimes it was just some corner of Athens he would dream of—that corner where Harmodios and Aristogeiton leaped out with their swords. Sometimes he would see the Akropolis, every temple of it and the beautiful statues.

Here in Sparta they had no beautiful statues of the gods. The Spartans had only the old statues which were shaped like pillars with head and arms stuck on them.

So at night Theras dreamed of Athens. But by

day he would not let the boys see his trouble or homesickness. He would not give the Spartans a chance to make fun of him.

Theras had been doing very well in the running matches and leaping. In these two acts he beat all the boys of the lochos. But one day he remembered that word of Hippias at the Isthmian Stadion, and Theras thought:

"I am leaping for the honour of Sparta," or "I am running this race all for Sparta, not for Athens, and when I go to the Isthmus or Olympia I will have to run or leap for Sparta's honour. Suppose I should run a race with an Athenian boy and beat him? Then I would actually bring shame upon my own town, Athens."

The thought sickened him. He could not run with any spirit, and in the midst of a leap he would think of this and fall short of the mark.

"What's the matter with you?" asked Drako one day. "You used to be the best in the lochos. Now Simmias and even Skyllis can beat you."

Theras was ashamed of this. "They will not beat me," he said to himself. "They shall not."

But he did not do any better, until once in the middle of the night he woke up.

"When I am big," he said to himself, "and when they take me to Olympia to run in the boys' races, I'll say to the whole crowd, the whole stadion, that I am an Athenian and that I am running for Athens's honour. Then if Hippias takes me out of the contest —let him do it."

After this Theras leaped and ran races better than ever.

One morning after the athletics Agis met him.

"Well," said Agis half tauntingly, "Sparta is not so bad after all, is it now?"

"No, not so bad," answered Theras, for he had learned Spartan obedience.

"Good as Athens, isn't it?"

Theras stopped still. The image of his own gymnasium in Athens suddenly rose in his mind. The cheerful merry boys, Klinias and the rest, his father coming to meet him and to take him home.

"Oh, no, no, no!" he suddenly burst out, forgetting Spartan discipline. "Sparta isn't anything like Athens. She is not fit to be a subject city of my Athens."

And unexpectedly he ran down the street, hiding his tears.

Agis looked puzzled and did not follow him.

CHAPTER XL

THE ARTEMIS VICTOR

ONE noon just as the boys finished their athletic practice, a company of Spartan men came into the Dromos to begin their exercise. They threw off their clothes and then Theras noticed one man who had terrible long scars on his back and shoulders. What had happened to that man! Theras stared and wondered, then seeing Drako starting toward the barracks, he ran to him. Drako would always answer his questions and was always kind. It was Drako who had given Theras the spear.

"Drako," he asked, "who is that soldier with the big scars? He must have been in a big battle. But what a strange place to get wounded—his back and shoulders."

"Oh, he's never been in a battle," answered Drako. "That's Strepon. He's an Artemis victor. We're very proud of him."

"An Artemis victor? What is that?"

"What, don't you have Artemis victors in Athens? What a strange place it must be!"

"But what is it?" persisted Theras.

"Well, you see, we Spartans have the most famous image of Artemis in the world. She is called Artemis Othia and is the very image which Iphigenia brought back from Tauris. While the image was in Tauris they offered human victims to her. So now she likes human blood. Every year a number of boys are flogged before her altar until the blood flows. The boy who can stand up the longest under the flogging is the victor and wins the Artemis crown. Strepon was flogged a long while ago, but the scars stay."

"Flogged before everybody?" questioned Theras, with staring eyes. "Just *whipped*, do you mean?"

"Yes, whipped with a long whip having metal thongs on the end that made deep cuts."

"How disgraceful!" broke out Theras. "I wouldn't stand up to be whipped like a slave."

"Hush—Artemis will hear you!"

"I don't care if she does. I don't believe the goddess Artemis wants people whipped. In Athens she never asks it. She only asks for the toys and dolls of little girls. She's a good goddess, not a horrid one like that!"

"All right, you go and see her. Then you'll know."

"But where is she?" persisted Theras.

"Down that way," said Drako, pointing southward. "Two miles down the road at Amyklai."

Theras wanted to see that dreadful image of Artemis. He could not help thinking about her—such a cruel goddess that wanted boys to be whipped until the blood ran.

Late that afternoon, as the ranks broke up from drill, Theras saw his chance and hurried off toward Amyklai. The captain never thought of any boy walking off like that without leave. He did not notice Theras. As for Theras, he was so tired of obeying so many commands all the time that he was glad to get away if only for an hour.

Soon he was by himself on the Amyklai road, whistling as he walked along.

CHAPTER XLI

A Shepherd Boy

It was toward sundown when Theras came to the Artemis shrine. There was a poor little temple beside the road. Within, so it could be seen from the open doorway, stood the image—a terrible one indeed—tall and straight like a post, made of painted wood, with stiff doll-like arms and the ugliest face Theras had ever seen. It had staring, greedy eyes, mouth like a slit, and high-bridged nose.

A priestess in a yellow dress was busy in the temple.

"What do you want, little boy?" she demanded. "Do you want to be whipped for Artemis? Come here and I'll whip you!"

"No, no," whispered Theras, backing out of the temple.

Once in the road again he ran as fast as his legs could carry him. But not toward Sparta. Captain Agis would catch him soon enough without that. He ran southward, farther away—where lay the open fields. These reminded him of his father's farm on Hymettos. To be sure, these were flat fields, while Pheidon's farm was hilly, but here the wheat grew tall and yellow, and smelt as sweet as at home in Attica. Beyond the wheat was a broad meadow of green cropped grass. In the midst of this Theras saw in the sunset light a flock of woolly sheep and a shepherd boy driving them. The boy had a double pipe to his mouth, and as he walked he piped a gay marching tune.

Theras hurried across the field toward him, and as he came up the boy stopped piping and made his mouth into such a round O of astonishment that Theras burst out laughing.

"Great Hermes, where did ye drop from?" said the boy. "Are ye sole alone?"

"I came from Sparta," laughed Theras, "and, the gods be thanked, I am alone."

"But why for? Did ye run away?"

"Yes, I did run away," answered Theras.

"Whew!" whistled the boy. "I wouldn't want to take the whipping you'll get."

"Well, I'm not going to get it till late to-night," declared Theras. "I'm not going to think about it now."

The boy looked at Theras, admiring him.

"Who be ye?" he asked.

"They call me the son of Hippias, but I'm not. I'm Pheidon's son, Theras, and I come from Athens."

"From Athens, be ye?" wondered the boy, gazing at Theras again. "I thought ye looked no Spartan. What made ye come down hither?"

"To see the terrible image," said Theras, lowering his voice, "the image that cries for blood."

"Cries for blood—nonsense," quoth the boy. "It's the Spartan cries for blood, not the image."

"How do you know?" asked Theras.

"Because it was our image or ever it were the Spartans'. We knew her before she ever went to the Tauric land. Artemis is kind, especially to hunters. If ye pray to her she'll give ye hunter's luck."

"She's kind in Athens too," declared Theras. "All she asks for is little girls' toys when they are all done with them."

"Of course, of course. Ye needn't be no feared of her," said the boy. "An' she's kind to animals big and little. There's my dog Kairos. He was terrible sick, he was. Just a puppy an' dyin' in my arms. An' I carried him to Artemis and prayed her help. From that very day the puppy got well. Where's that dog? Here, Kairos, you rascal! Here!"

From a little copse came running a rough hound. He growled and bristled as he saw Theras.

"Keep still," cried the boy. "Theras is all right. Now 'tend to yer own business, Kairos. Go on, Kairos."

Thus commanded, the dog ran ahead, started the sheep up from where they had begun to graze, and began to drive them along.

"See how smart he is," said the boy proudly. "We'd better follow him. It's time to go home. You come along too." Then as Theras hesitated, "Come on to supper, and after I'll see ye pieceway toward Sparta."

So Theras went. The boy took out his shepherd flute again and began to play a wild, bright marching tune, and to this tune the two stepped along, driving the sheep.

Why is it that sometimes two boys, the minute they meet, are chums, while two other boys will take a year to get acquainted, fighting all the time just like two young roosters?

Theras, as he walked along with this boy, felt as if he had known him always, like the boys in the Athens school. He even wanted to tell him all the things he had kept secret from the boys in Sparta, and all this even though the boy was a slave—or Theras thought he was a slave.

CHAPTER XLII

THE PERIOIKOI OF SPARTA

THEY kept walking across the fields and soon they came upon a farmhouse with the sheepfold and haystacks near.

"Mother," called the boy, "I've brought a boy home to supper."

"Which one?" called back a cheery voice from the house.

"Oh, a stranger!"

Instantly the mother appeared at the doorway—such a frightened face.

"Who is it, Abas?" she asked her son. "Where did you meet him?"

"Oh, he's all right, Mother," answered the boy Abas easily. "Talk to him—you'll see," and he hurried away to fold the sheep.

The woman looked at Theras sharply.

"Why did ye come out hither?" she asked.

"Because I've been in Sparta so many weeks I couldn't stand it any longer, at least not to-day," laughed Theras.

It was astonishing how the woman's face cleared, for Theras spoke the speech of Athens, not of Sparta.

"Ay, I see ye are no Spartan," she said. "Come, lad, come in to sup with us. Abas," she called, "Hæmon, Father—supper's ready."

A bent, hard-worked man and a youth splendidly tall came from beyond the hayricks.

They all went into the house. It was a simple hut built of limestone, but it was fairly large, and as he entered Theras saw it had a second room at the back, which was unusual for slave houses. The table was loaded with the best dinner (so it seemed to Theras) that he had ever looked upon. Roast lamb, fresh goat's milk, good bread, dates, honey cakes, and wine. Theras was amazed. The father poured wine to the gods and they sat down.

"Hello," said the young man Hæmon, looking across at Theras. "That's the youngster old Hippias brought from Athens. I saw him the first day. Ye had a hard time in the drill, didn't ye; laddie?"

"Yes," answered Theras eagerly. "But I can do the drill now; I can indeed."

"I saw ye were quick to learn," said Hæmon kindly.

"Ye know him, then," said Dinarchos, the father. There was evident relief in his tone, as if somehow all of them had been afraid of Theras. Theras was glad to see that now they trusted him. He had occasion later on to be gladder yet of that trust.

What a fine young man Hæmon was, strong yet gentle. Theras had not seen manners like his since he had come to Sparta, and how was it that these simple shepherds, who must be slaves, should have so much of everything?

Before Theras thought, he spoke:

"But are you slaves?" he asked wonderingly. "How

can you be slaves?" They all answered at once and with some heat:

"Slaves! Of course not. No, no, no."

Theras blushed scarlet and rising made a little bow as a polite Athenian boy should do.

"Forgive me, please," he said. "Of course, I should have known you are metics."

"Metics," cried the old man. "We are not *metics*."

He seemed almost angrier at the word "metic" than at the word "slave." For a metic always came from far away and could never be a full-righted citizen.

"Nay, tell the laddie the right of it," spoke up the mother kindly. "Coming from Athens, mayhap he's never heard of the like of us." She smiled at Theras mother-fashion.

"We be *Perioikoi*," explained Hæmon. "At least the Spartans call us that, meaning we 'dwell near.' But really we have always lived in this land, we and our fathers afore us. We be Achæans. The land was ours or ever the Spartan came." Hæmon began to speak very low.

"They took away our cities and our rights from us," he whispered. "But they could never take the land. They would starve quickly enough, those Spartans, if they drove us from our farms."

"Hush, hush, Hæmon," said his mother in fear. "Have ye no prudence at all! Nay, guest-laddie,"—this to Theras—"sit ye down again. Why, ye've finished everything on yer plate. Ay, but they starve ye—those Spartans—that I know. Give him more, Father, more of everything."

"Ay, Baukis, that I will."

So Dinarchos heaped Theras's plate again, while Abas hastened to give him more honey cakes.

"Tell us of your home, lad," said Dinarchos. "Tell of your own folk and how it was ye came away from them so far."

Theras had not been so happy since he had left his dear Athens.

CHAPTER XLIII

A Strange Arrest

They were all cosily eating their supper and Theras was talking, when Dinarchos lifted both his hands, crying sharply:

"What is that?" In the silence they all heard footsteps on the turf outside.

Theras guessed at once that the Spartans had come for him, and like a flash he dived into the farther room. There he had just time to hide behind some cloaks hanging on the wall, when the front room was filled with armed men.

The poor mother, Baukis, gave a stifled cry. But not one of the family spoke or moved.

"I wonder if they'll tell," thought Theras. "I wonder if those Spartans will hurt them because I am here. If I could only get out——"

Theras peeped from the folds of the cloak and saw

A STRANGE ARREST

Strepon, the Artemis victor, standing in the lighted room, saw other armed Spartans. Strange that Agis, his own captain, should not be there.

"Dinarchos," spoke Strepon, "we have come to do you honour. Your son, Hæmon, has performed a brave deed which we cannot forget."

Again Baukis gave that little heartbroken cry and clapped her hand over her own mouth. Hæmon rose, very serious and tall, looking at the men.

Dinarchos, too, rose from his seat.

Theras began to wonder what it was all about.

"Ye Spartans," said Dinarchos, "we have no wish for honours. We wish only to keep to our farm work. We killed a sheep to-day. Belike ye will accept the mutton from us. We have eaten only a little of it."

Theras was still more puzzled. He leaned a little farther from his hiding-place. Could it be that the Spartans had not come for him, after all? They seemed to be doing some kindness to Hæmon. Why then were all the family so unwilling, so angry, so frightened?

"Nay, Father," Hæmon was saying, "why tell them of the sheep? It is enough that they take me."

"Have you no thanks for the honour we pay you?" asked Strepon with a queer smile. "You saved a freeborn Spartan from death. Behold your crown."

He lifted a crown of laurel and stepped toward Hæmon. Hæmon, like a flash, struck the crown out of Strepon's hand.

"You shall not crown me, you liar," he said. "Do to me what you are going to do and stop pretending."

Then Hæmon leaned over to his father, kissed him good-bye, kissed his mother and Abas.

All three began to cry bitterly, but Hæmon did not weep. He stepped forward to the Spartans and with them went away into the night.

CHAPTER XLIV

A Youth too Brave

Theras in his hiding-place did not know what to do. Dinarchos, Baukis, and Abas had all forgotten him. They were weeping together and kept calling Hæmon's name.

"We shall never see him again. Never, never," they said. "We shall never see Hæmon again!"

After a while Theras stole out and touched Abas's hand.

"I am going now. I must go back to Sparta."

"I'll go with you," responded Abas quickly. He was glad to get away from all the weeping and sorrow.

The two boys were soon out on the Spartan road in the starlight.

"Don't cry, Abas," said Theras. "Surely you will see Hæmon again. He's only gone to Sparta."

"No, no, he will not come back. That is the way the Spartans do. They have taken Hæmon away to kill him."

"To kill him! What on earth do you mean?"

"Yes, they'll kill him," repeated Abas, trying to keep back his sobs.

"But what has Hæmon done?"

"Only this. Last week, Kleon—he's a Spartan young man—and three others were up in the mountains, hunting. Kleon fell over a cliff. He caught a branch and was hanging there ready to tumble down into the gorge, a hundred feet down. He screamed like anything for help, but none of the other fellows went down after him. They'd get to the edge and balk. But Hæmon crept down to him. He's like a cat, Hæmon is." Here Abas began to sob again. "Hæmon helped Kleon to a ledge and then led him up the cliff. He saved Kleon's life."

"But, Abas, that was a good deed. They will never kill Hæmon for that."

"Yes, they will, they will," cried Abas. "They will not let a Perioikos, man or boy, be too brave for fear we will hurt Sparta. And if I grow up brave and splendid like Hæmon they will kill me too."

"No, no, they would not dare," said Theras, who could not bring himself to believe this thing. "You are not slaves."

"No, we be Perioikoi," asserted Abas, lifting up his head. "The Spartans do not often treat us Perioikoi so. But Hæmon was proud and beautiful. He was brave where the Spartans failed. They won't stand that." Then he added in a whisper, "It's the Helots they usually treat so. The Spartans have a secret organisation called the *Cryptia*. The *Cryptia* go everywhere spying. If a Helot disobeys, or even if he is too clever, they kill him. But me also will they spy upon, because of Hæmon. If I had anywhere to go I would run away."

"I'm going to run away some day," answered Theras, suddenly remembering his old resolve. "But I must be older and stronger. If I should run away now someone would steal me for a slave. There are lots of slave thieves on the roads."

"Yes, yes, I know," said Abas fearfully.

By this time Theras and Abas had come to the first houses of Sparta.

"Good-bye," said Abas. "I must go back now quick. See, yonder is a sentinel."

"I'll come to see you again, Abas," said Theras. "Pretty soon I'll come. And if I see Hæmon in Sparta I'll tell him to hurry back home."

But Abas was already disappearing down the road.

A moment later the sentinel caught Theras, shook him, and marched him off to his barracks.

Here Agis gave Theras a great thrashing.

"But never mind," thought Theras when it was over. "It was worth a thrashing to get away like that."

Theras kept remembering that happy evening in the home of the Perioikoi. Happy for him, yet so unhappy for them. But Theras did not believe Hæmon would be killed. The Spartans would not be so foolish and unreasonable as that. If the Spartans had purposed to kill Hæmon, surely they would have taken him roughly from his home. But they had brought Hæmon a crown. They had treated him kindly.

Still the thing kept coming back to Theras. And at night he dreamed of Hæmon's kind face.

CHAPTER XLV

PLATANISTOS

To Theras all Spartan days were alike. To the Spartan boys this was not so. They were always talking about some celebration, or festival, or procession that was coming soon. Now they began to talk of Platanistos.

"Is Platanistos a festival?" asked Theras.

The boys nudged each other and laughed. "No, Kora dear," Skyllis answered mockingly.

"Is it a procession?"

"No, and yet part of it is a procession."

"Is it in honour of some god?"

"No—unless the god is Ares."

"Stop your kidding," said Drako. "You come with me, Theras, I'll tell you.

"They kid you because they're jealous," Drako continued, as the two walked along. "You've beat them all at the long jump for a week past. I will tell you. Platanistos is a battle. All the bigger boys are in it. I'm going to be in it because I'm old enough. I'm older than you other boys in the lochos."

Drako looked proud as he said this.

"A battle?" questioned Theras. "A real battle? Do you have real spears?"

"No. That's just it. We have no spears, nor any weapons at all. We have to show what we can do with just ourselves, our two hands and feet and teeth."

All this seemed to Theras very grand and brave.

Several times that week Theras asked after Hæmon, but nobody seemed to know anything about Hæmon. Nobody talked of anything but Platanistos.

At last the day arrived. Never had Theras seen the Spartan boys so excited. Early in the afternoon the two companies, or teams of fighters, marched down the Apheta Way and out on the southern road. All the town—men, boys, and even women—went hurrying after them in the dust. All the boys were shouting:

"Go it, Herakleans," or

"Go it, Lycurgians."

For these were the names of the two contending teams.

Soon they came to a field where some plane trees grew. This field was surrounded by a wide brook, so once within the field no boy could get away. It was a small island. The townspeople stood on the outside bank of the brook. But the teams of fighters marched over the bridges into the Plane Tree Island, each team over its own bridge.

The two teams stood in order, like little armies facing each other. Then the leader yelled "Go!"

And with a terrific shout, the two armies of boys flew at each other.

Theras, standing at the brook's edge, saw it all.

Great Hermes, what a splendid brave fight—fists, kicks, jumping, and yelling. Theras yelled with them, cheering on his team.

Suddenly above the din there was a shriek of pain. A big boy had sprung upon Drako and was gouging at his eyes. He seemed to forget that this was a game.

"Stop him!" cried Theras. "Stop him! He's killing Drako—killing Drako!"

But no one paid any heed.

Then Drako fell. To fall was to be trampled upon instantly and killed.

Theras jerked the skirt of the man standing near. "Stop them! Quick, quick! Save Drako," he pleaded. But the man shook him off with an oath.

"What's the matter, little fool? Leave me alone."

Then Theras threw himself desperately into the stream, swimming to the fighters. He forgot he was too little. He only thought he must help Drako. But the man dashed after him, pulled him ashore, and fell to pummelling him as Theras had never been pummelled in his life.

"You young rat," he howled, "what do you mean, interfering with Platanistos? Don't you know Platanistos is sacred? You—you—you hound!"

The Spartan seemed in a sort of madness, as though the cruelty of Platanistos was in him.

"But Drako will be killed," Theras managed to stutter out between blows.

"Killed! Of course he's killed. He'd no business to fall. Do we want a boy that *fell* in Platanistos!"

Suddenly a wilder howl of joy from the bystanders

caught the man's attention. And in that moment Theras wrenched himself free and ran wildly away. Bruised, bleeding, breathless, he ran on and on until the mad, cruel noise was faint and far behind.

He was running from *that* rather than from the whipping. "Drako was killed. Drako was killed." That terrible thing seemed to fasten fangs into his heart.

Theras could not know that by some incredible luck Drako had been kicked backward out of the worst press of the fighters. Then he had struggled to his feet. He was wonderfully quick, was Drako. It was this which had won him admittance to those highly honoured ranks of Platanistos. But on the outer edge of the fighters he could not force himself into it again.

So Drako was saved. Two boys were killed in the fight that day, but Drako was not one of them.

But all this Theras did not know. The Spartan, too, had thought Drako was killed.

CHAPTER XLVI

A Cruel Deed

Theras ran and ran. He did not think at all whither he was running. He thought only of Drako, Drako.

How cruelly the Spartans had killed him!

At last tired out, aching all over from the man's beating, damp from his plunge in the stream, Theras

A CRUEL DEED

sank down by the roadside. He did not know how long he had sat there, when at last looking up he noticed that it was growing dark. The sun had set and the mists were stealing over the fields.

Time to go back to the barracks.

Theras jumped to his feet, saying quite aloud, "I *won't* go back to the barracks. I won't go back to Sparta. I won't go back where they kill their own boys for fun."

Oh, how Theras hated Sparta! How he despised everything about it. Athens! Why, Athens was a very heaven compared to Sparta. Theras did not know that the reason for his hating Sparta was because he hated to be a brute-savage.

Sparta, in spite of her laws, her military drill (the best in the world), her splendid, fearless, beautiful men, was really a savage state.

But Athens was civilised.

That means that the Athenians were just and reasonable, and loved other things rather than fighting and bloodshed. Athenians also were free to think and speak out, but the Spartans did not dare to think or to speak what they thought.

Theras could not explain all this. He only kept shuddering as he thought of Drako, and how he had been killed with cruel joy.

Suddenly Theras remembered Hæmon. Yes, the Spartans had killed Hæmon too. How foolish Theras had been not to believe it. They had killed Hæmon and would kill Abas, if they could find any excuse. Abas!

"No, no, they shall not kill Abas. Not Abas too."

Then all at once a plan came to Theras. It came like a flash, as if Athena had given it.

Theras would run away from Sparta, not some other time but now—now! This very night; and he would take Abas with him. Those Spartans should not get Abas—no—no. Theras forgot to be afraid of slave-stealers on the road, or anything else.

He would go now.

He began to look around. Why there, down the road, was the Artemis temple. He could barely see it in the twilight. Yes, Platanistos itself was on the way to Amyklai. Theras had been running southward and was now not far away from Abas's home.

PART III.—A TOUGH JOURNEY

PART III
A TOUGH JOURNEY

CHAPTER XLVII

IN THE HAYSTACKS

THERAS ran swiftly along, keeping a little way from the road for fear of meeting someone. It was not long before he reached the little stone hut where Abas lived. He hid behind the haystacks. He was afraid to go in. Dinarchos and Baukis might send him back to Sparta. And what would they say about Abas going away? Surely they would say "No."

Theras must reach Abas alone. But how?

He crept nearer in the dark. Came to the sheepfold; an old ewe, seeing him, came up to the bars, *baa*-ing for food. Theras heard the dog Kairos in the house bark sharply,—heard Dinarchos's voice:

"Go, Abas—see what's up with the sheep."

And in a moment more Abas was there by the sheepfold.

"Abas, hush—be still—it's Theras, only Theras." Theras spoke quickly, for Abas jumped like a hare when he saw someone crouching in the dark.

"Theras! What are you doing? Why——"

But even while Abas was asking, Theras was pulling him by the arm away to the haystacks.

"Ss—t," said Theras. "I'm going to run away, Abas. Yes, this very night, and I want you to go with me."

Abas was so astonished that his eyes glittered even in the dark.

"Me?" he said. "Me? Run away? Where to?"

"To Athens. Oh, Abas, I'll take care of you in Athens. If you stay here, Abas, they'll kill you. The Spartans will kill you for certain."

"Oh, Artemis! Are they coming—now?"

Abas began to whimper with fear.

"No, no," whispered Theras, shaking him. "But some day, Abas. Just as you said. As soon as you get bigger. They've killed Drako in the Platanistos fight."

"Not Drako," began Abas, "I saw him this——"

"Yes, but they did. They killed him this afternoon. Oh, poor Drako."

Sobs came into Theras's throat, but he went on:

"They've killed Hæmon too. I've asked and asked and nobody has seen Hæmon. Abas, will you come?"

"By Zeus, I will!" answered Abas so suddenly that Theras shook him again for very relief and joy.

"Will they let you go—Baukis and Dinarchos?" he asked. "Will they let you go?"

"Mother would let me, but Father will say I must stay and help with the farm."

"What shall we do? Not tell either of them?"

"No—I must tell Mother," said Abas. "Perhaps Father'll go to bed. You wait here for me."

For Dinarchos was already peering out of the door and calling fretfully:

THE PARTING

"You rascal, Abas, what are you doing out there so long?"

Abas hurried into the lighted doorway. Theras hid himself in the stack and waited.

Moments passed—a half-hour, an hour. He could hear Dinarchos's voice growling along. Would he never go to bed? Why did not Abas come out? Suppose Abas should be stupid and let out the secret by mistake?

Theras's hands grew cold as he thought this.

If it got too late, he'd have to go alone. He couldn't wait all night and let the Spartans come for him. Theras got up and shook off the hay.

Must he go alone, indeed?

CHAPTER XLVIII

THE PARTING

JUST then the doorway darkened and out came Baukis and Abas.

Baukis was talking in puzzled whispers:

"Why should I come out, lad? Father's gone abed an' we must go too. What is it you want to tell me?"

"Theras is out here," said Abas.

"Theras—why?"

Theras hurried to them.

"You ask her," said Abas breathlessly.

So Theras told in whispers about Drako and how

he himself wanted to run away to Athens and take Abas with him, so that Abas should not be killed also.

Poor Baukis put her hands to her head, all in a fright and puzzle.

"Who's goin' to kill Abas? Who?" she demanded.

"Nobody now, Mother," said Abas. "But the Spartans will, some day, you know they will."

Baukis turned angrily to Theras.

"Whatever made ye come, puttin' notions into my boy's head?"

"It isn't a notion, Baukis. Abas thought of it the night they took Hæmon."

At the word "Hæmon" a low moan came from Baukis.

"Ye're too little, laddies," she pleaded, "too little, the both of ye, to run away."

"If we wait till we're big it will be too late," spoke Abas.

Baukis shook her finger threateningly in Theras's face. "If they catch *ye*, lad, they'll kill ye. You— yes, certainer than they'd kill my boy. Ye'd best go back to Sparta, ye had."

"I won't go back, I won't," said Theras, though her threat frightened him.

Baukis began to walk to and fro just, so Theras thought, as if someone were prodding her with a spear and she trying to get out of the way. She kept talking to herself:

"The lad can't go. Sure to be killed. What'll Dinarchos say? Oh—oh. No, no, no." And she would shake her head.

THE PARTING

The boys did not know what to think of her.

Suddenly she stopped in front of Theras.

"What can ye do for my boy in Athens, now? I ask ye that!"

"I can take him to Epikides or some other friend of my father's. I will tell them to make him a freed-man."

"How'll ye get to Athens?"

"Oh, Baukis, I can remember most of the road. I'll ask the way."

"Ay-ay, an' get taken by the first slave thief that meets ye. Now look ahere, lads. Ye'll go by no high-road. Ye'll go first up Mount Taÿgetos past Erysthenes's farm an' on up to Bion's house, then turn to the north—ye know the way, Abas—and when morning dawns ye'll come to Bion's son's house. Bion's son is a true man and brave. Bide with him for the day and he will show ye the way to the next farm. So shall ye go from farm to farm, an' each man will show ye farther till ye get so far from Sparta that they cannot catch ye."

Something seemed to catch back Baukis's voice.

"Wait here—ye must have bread," she said, and ran fast into the house.

The boys looked at each other.

"I believe she's letting me go," said Abas.

"She never said 'yes,' but she's doing it," answered Theras.

In a short time Baukis came out again with a fat little bundle and two cloaks. She gave them to Abas, kissed him, and hugged him tight.

"Never see ye again," she whispered. "Never, never! I'll pray Artemis for ye and sacrifice to her. Now hurry!"

And she pushed Abas off. But as she turned away, bent almost double and head low, Theras felt so strange and full of sorrow that he ran to her and threw both arms about her neck, kissing her as though she were his own mother in Athens.

CHAPTER XLIX

IN TAŸGETOS MOUNTAINS

IN the darkness the two boys walked as fast as they could toward the mountains. They were anxious to get out of the open fields where some Spartan soldiers might spy them. They did not speak a word. Abas, scared to death, would not let Theras know it, and Theras, scared for his life, would not tell Abas. So between them they kept their courage up.

At last they came to the steep hillsides of Taÿgetos, and fairly plunged into the forest. How like a cloak it felt to protect them! Abas had led the way to the bed of a little stream, and up the side of this they began to clamber. In the forest it was black darkness. They could hardly see a foot in front of them. The way was not so steep at first, but soon it was hand over hand, stumble and tumble, and a bruised knee for Theras. Abas climbed better than Theras could.

"How can you tell where to go?" asked Theras. "It's dark as a peddler's pocket."

Bang! Down went Abas against a sharp stone and stopped to hold his foot tight, rocking to and fro.

"Let's stop awhile," he said. "We've come pretty far. The moon should rise soon. Then we'll go better."

So they sat there on the rocks.

How damp it was and cold!

They wrapped themselves in Baukis's two cloaks, which were none too warm.

A twig cracked close to them. They could not hear steps, but somehow they knew that something was stepping, stealing along near them.

"What's that?" whispered Theras.

"Perhaps an otter or a fox coming to drink," said Abas. Of course, he knew that it might be a wildcat, but he would not say so.

Whatever it was, it splashed into the water, and they could hear the *lap-lap* of its tongue while it drank. Suddenly with a great *scatter-scamper* it ran away.

"It scented us," said Abas.

They were glad to be still again.

But it was not for long. Again the bushes cracked and snapped.

Something was coming this time by leaps and bounds.

The boys jumped to their feet.

"The soldiers," said Theras.

"No, an animal," said Abas, who was more used to the woods. "Don't you hear it sniffing along the ground?"

But both boys knew that the Spartans might easily come out after them with hounds.

"Quick—here's a tree," cried Abas. "Climb up after me."

But before even Abas could clamber far, a dog leaped upon them.

What did he do, that dog, but break out into joyous whines and barks, like a person crying for joy, springing up to Abas, licking his feet?

Abas tumbled out of the tree.

"It's Kairos!" cried he. "Good old Kairos. You did find us, didn't you? You wouldn't let us go alone, good old Kairos."

Both boys began to pat the dog's head and sides as if they had not seen him for a year. As for Kairos, he nearly wagged his tail off.

"You know, he'll be fine to have with us," said Abas proudly. "He can hunt hares, and I can skin them and cook them. Hæmon showed me how."

But at the word "Hæmon" both boys longed to hurry on.

"There's the moon!" cried Abas. "See the light through the trees."

And at that the boys and dog began to clamber up the hillside as fast as ever they could.

CHAPTER L

IN THE NIGHT

It was after midnight when they came to a broad platform of rock half-way up the mountains. Here was a cluster of houses, ten or twelve.

"There's Bion's house," said Abas, pointing. "And here—yes, here is the little path."

So in the flecked and chequered moonlight under the great solemn, quiet trees, the two boys plodded on, and Kairos kept soberly with them.

They were too excited to be tired from their climb. For hours they walked or clambered, and though their legs began to ache and their eyes to feel strange and twitchy, neither boy would have thought of stopping. They both knew that on this first night they must get as far as possible from Sparta.

At length Theras began to realise that he could see quite a long way through the wood. And a sweet fresh smell came up from the mould. Then a breeze just suddenly started from nowhere through the forest, brisk and busy, stirring the branches.

"It's morning," said Abas. "Whew, but I'm glad. I wish we'd get to Bion's house."

Then at a sudden turn there was Bion's house indeed, closed and asleep.

But the two farm dogs were not asleep. With wild howls and barks up they sprang. They started for Theras, then seeing Kairos jumped upon him. Instantly the three dogs were rolling over each other, yelping and hissing and squealing.

"Bion!" called Abas, "Bion, come out. Quick."

He jumped into the midst of the dogs to save Kairos, and Theras sprang to help him.

When Father Bionides stumbled out of his door he saw just a whirling confusion of boys, dogs, boy legs and dog tails, and heard the screeching barks and the hoarse dog-swearing which dogs keep up when they fight, all mixed together.

At first Bion hoped his dogs would eat up the travellers who came prowling at such an hour, then seeing that they were only young boys he ran forward.

"Gê, come off; Cerberus, here—here!" and he pulled back his dogs while Abas got Kairos into his arms.

"Now, what do you boys want here?" demanded Bion angrily.

"Bion, I am Abas. Mother sent this to you to show she sent me," and Abas drew from his belt a piece of finely woven cloth, a gay pattern which only Baukis could make. "See?" he said.

"That's so. That be Baukis's weaving," said Bion. "But why did ye come?"

Abas was silent. He was afraid to tell.

"Bion," spoke up Theras, "did you know about Hæmon?"

"I know Hæmon, yes. What about him?"

"The Spartans killed him. We don't want Abas killed too."

IN THE NIGHT

"Hæmon! Hæmon killed! Great Zeus!"

Bion's face darkened with anxiety.

"We want you to hide us for to-day in your house," said Theras.

"No, I won't hide ye in my house. I'll do better nor that. Come with me."

He led the way to the back of his hut and up the hill to a small cave almost hidden by undergrowth.

"Bide ye here," he said kindly. "I'll call ye when to go." And he left them.

There they were at last.

The boys took a long breath and sat down. Abas opened his mother's bundle, showing a big loaf of black bread, some goat cheese, figs, and even honey cakes.

Both fell upon these like two young wolves. Never had anything tasted so good.

When it was half gone, Theras said:

"Ought we not to save the rest for to-morrow?"

"Yes," sighed Abas. "But I could eat all of it and that much again."

"So could I," said Theras. "But we mustn't."

So they folded up the bundle and lay down in the cave.

Outside in the forest a thrush began to sing its long, sweet morning song.

Suddenly the thought came to Theras as he lay there: "I am going back to Athens. I am really going. In a week, or maybe two weeks, I'll see the streets, the temples, the houses, my house, and Mother!"

It seemed as if this were the first moment of

knowing it. The surprise made his heart jump and his throat ache as if he were going to cry.

But he did not cry—instead, he went to sleep without even turning over.

CHAPTER LI

THE SPARTANS PURSUE

ABOUT five minutes later, so it seemed to Theras, he was wakened by something, he knew not what. Afternoon shadows lay outside at the mouth of the cave and the level beams of sunset.

Voices had awakened him. Not loud voices. It must have been that Theras was fearful and wary even in his sleep. That was why he woke so easily. He crept to the mouth of the cave and peered through the bushes down on Bion's hut.

Great Zeus! There were men all about the hut— Spartans! The Spartans had found them! Yes, there was Agis, the captain. It was Agis talking:

"Now, Bion, are you sure you have not seen the boy? You know what will happen to you if you lie to me."

This was a threat.

"Why should I lie, sir? What is it to me?" said Bion.

"Well, we shall search your hut."

THE SPARTANS PURSUE 143

"All right. You are welcome to do so."

Theras froze with horror. Suppose Bion had taken them to his hut as they had asked him to do! Like a flash, Theras was back into the farthest part of the cave. There was Abas still asleep. Should he wake him and run? But how? They were in far more danger of being caught if they tried to run away. No, they would stay in the cave. Abas was hidden behind a curve of the cave wall. Theras hid too. He could still hear the voices.

"Well, he's not in the hut," came Agis's disappointed voice.

"Where do you think the boy was going?" inquired Bion.

"Theras? To Athens, of course."

"Well, then, sir, excuse me for asking, but why do ye search for him here?"

"Because someone saw him last night running down the Amyklai road, and old Hippias would have it that we must search the mountains. A fool's errand, I say. Of course, others are searching the Athens road. That's where they'll find him."

"Oh, it's that Athenian boy ye're after. I've heard of him."

Theras caught his breath again. Oh, if they would only go, those Spartans!

But they kept stamping restlessly around the hut.

"We lost our hounds," Agis said. "They scented a fox and took after him like mad. We've given them the scent of the boy, though, so if he were here the hounds would find him."

Theras could feel his hair lifting and creeping on his head. His teeth began to chatter. He had never been so afraid before, not even when the toy-man had him.

"Yes, those hound dogs are pretty sure," he heard Bion's voice. How easy and slow Bion was, as if he really knew nothing about the boys.

"Well — good - bye, Bion," said Agis suddenly. "We'll go back to Sparta. But remember, if Theras comes this way and you catch him for us, we'll reward you."

They hurried off. Oh, how good to hear those retreating footsteps! How still it was now! Nothing but birds twittering. But the dogs! What should he do? Stay here, or make a dash away? He could not decide, and the dark hiding-place seemed so good that he had not the courage to come out.

Suddenly footsteps were at the mouth of the cave. Bion! Suppose, oh, suppose Bion were to catch him for the reward!

Bion came in, a pitcher in his hands.

"Lads," he said, peering in the dark, "wake up." He leaned, shaking Abas. "Wake up, I say."

"Those Spartans," spoke Theras, trembling, "are they gone? Do you think they are really gone?"

"I don't know, but I think so. Anyhow, ye must get away from here as quick as may be. I'm more afraid of the hounds than of the Spartans. Here, drink this milk an' come!"

He poured the good goat's milk into a bowl and the boys drank, hardly tasting it.

THE SPARTANS PURSUE 145

"What's the matter?" Abas kept asking. "What about dogs?"

"Nothing," said Bion. "Only ye must get away. Now *hurry*. I'm going with ye."

Again the fear crossed Theras. Would Bion take them back to Sparta?

Bion led them up away from his hut and toward the north—the way they wished to go. But why, why had he come with them? Theras was more and more anxious. Agis had promised Bion a reward!

Presently they came to a little stream, dashing and singing down the hillside.

"Now, lads," said Bion, "ye can thank the nymph of this stream for saving ye. Get into the stream, sandals and all, and walk down it—yes, toward Sparta. But ye are north of Sparta now. This way ye will wash off the scent and the dogs can't track ye. An' I hope the Spartans won't track ye, either. There's a real good road higher on the mountain. The Spartans will expect ye to take that. Go down and fool them. Abas, ye can find the sheep-path—it's by a big, crooked pine tree, an' just beyond it the brook takes a turn. Watch for it and hurry, both of ye.

"The farther ye can get to-night, the better it'll be for ye. Ye will get to Lycurgus's hut, but if ye can, go farther on to Nikias's. Get as far away as ye can."

Bion explained to Abas about the path, then thrust into Theras's hand a little piece of wood carved with a rude picture of a goat.

"Nikias will know that mark of mine," he said. "Ye keep it. It's *ye* they are after, not Abas."

And so he left them.

The boys hurried off, splashing down the stream. They did not stop even to thank Bion. Theras only felt immense relief that Bion was not going to hurt them.

The twilight helped them now or they could never have found their way down the rough stream-bed.

"There's a crooked pine," said Abas at last. "And yes, the brook turns yonder. Wait—yes—here's the sheep-path."

And they hurried on.

No, they did not thank Bion, but Theras all his life remembered that the poor man in his mountain hut would not take money to betray two little boys to the Spartans.

Good, honest Bion! Yes, all his life Theras remembered him and thanked him.

CHAPTER LII

Forest Journeys

Night fell as they hurried through the woods. Faithful Kairos was with them, trotting silent at their heels. He had followed them splashing down the stream. Kairos got along all right in the pitch dark. But the boys could neither see their path nor get forward without constant stumbling.

So they sat down in the dark to wait. At every sound they thought they heard the hounds baying, and when a fox barked they both jumped to their feet in terror. To be chased by hounds is the most frightening of all chasing. The boys knew the hounds could smell their footsteps on the path, and if they once found the footsteps could find them too.

"Oh," said Abas, springing to his feet, "I wish —I wish I hadn't come."

"Yes," thought Theras, "if I hadn't brought Abas out he would have been safe at home."

Then he spoke out:

"Do you want to go back, Abas? You can go back to Bion's house. Bion said the Spartans were not after you."

Abas hesitated. But the idea of going off and leaving Theras alone made him ashamed.

"No, I won't go back," he said. "I won't. I knew we'd have trouble before I came. I'm sorry I said that, Theras."

So they waited in silence.

Would the moon never rise? And every moment was so precious for hurrying away from Sparta. Sparta was yet too near, much too near.

At last, slowly, the large bright disc appeared so silently in the sky. The light trickled into the forest. Branches here and there caught the silvery gleam. The leaves seemed polished and glittering.

The boys had wandered off the path. But they soon found it again and hastened along it, out of breath.

When they came to a hut they circled far around

it, for fear of arousing the farm dogs. Long after midnight they came to Lycurgus's hut.

"Let's try to go onward to Nikias's," whispered Theras.

"It will be full daylight when we get there," said Abas.

"Never mind. Let's try it, anyway."

And the tired feet pushed on along the path. Sure enough, the sun rose and climbed the sky in splendour. Still Nikias's hut came not in sight.

"Never mind," said Theras. "We're farther away from Sparta. We're farther away."

And when he said it new strength seemed to come into his back and he could walk fast again.

But it was two very, very weary boys who reached Nikias's hut at mid-morning.

Theras showed his goat picture and Nikias received them kindly and took them out to a ruined sheepfold, where they slept.

That evening Nikias told them the way to the city of Orestium, which would be their next stop.

Then once more they were on the mountain path —so endless in its ups and downs, in its rocky turns, its sudden views of the Laconian valley far, far down below them, still catching the faded light. This path was higher up the mountain and the trees were low and scraggy.

On this night's journey they were to pass the boundary line of Laconia, the Spartan country, and come into the country of Arkadia.

"Do you think we have passed it yet?" Theras

FOREST JOURNEYS

kept asking. Oh, the joy to be out of the Spartan country!

At last in the dawning light they came upon a tiny river pouring down from mountain heights.

Nikias had told them they would find it. It was the River Alpheus. Now the boys knew they were in Arkadia.

"We are in Arkadia. We're in Arkadia!" said Theras thankfully. He knelt, trembling, upon the bank to drink. He was very tired and his feet and ankles ached. It seemed a wonderful blessing just to stop.

"Let's rest here a moment," he said.

"We'd better keep going," answered Abas. "We must reach Orestium."

But Abas, too, was so tired that he sat down beside Theras and gazed into the stream.

"I wish we were going to follow the Alpheus and come to Olympia," said Abas. "I want to see the stadion where the men and boys run races."

"But I only want to go to Athens," answered Theras. "Only to Athens. And oh, Abas, when we get there! As soon as I have seen Mother and Aglaia and Opis, I will go straight for Epikides. He is so kind! I will ask him to help you, to find some work for you. But you shall live at our house. And I know Epikides will make you a freed-man. I'll ask him that first of all."

So the two boys sat by the famous Alpheus River and planned their homecoming. Little did they think how far away was Athens still, and how long and dangerous the way.

CHAPTER LIII

A Prayer to Pan

NEAR Orestium they stopped at the hut of another shepherd named Leon. All these shepherds and farmers were Perioikoi, as Abas was, and knew each other.

The boys were not following the usual road to Athens. If you will look at the map you will see how far out of the way they came. No Spartan would think of searching for them up here in Arkadia. At least, unless some Perioikos told the Spartans where to look. So Theras suggested that they might now, from Orestium on, make their journeys by day.

Happy they were as they started out from the Arkadian city at sunrise. So free it seemed to be walking in the daylight instead of at night. The little houses and temples of Orestium, clinging to hillsides or half hidden in glens, were all shining in the morning sun.

So they went forth into a world of mountains. Mountains near, towering with snowy peaks into the sky; mountains afar, stretching away and away into a very dream of mountains. For Arkadia is all hills in every direction.

There were few trees. On the bare mountains and hills the light rested rosy red, golden, purple in the distances, until the world seemed dipped in a great mist or sea of colour.

A PRAYER TO PAN

Last night both boys had been footsore, and their sandals, worn to shreds, fairly flapped off their feet. But the good Leon of Orestium had given them some half-worn sandals belonging to his own son, and now in the morning all the footsoreness and backaches were gone.

Theras skipped along the mountain road singing, for singing was an Athenian boy's whistling. And he was happy.

Kairos, too, was happy and kept darting in and out of bushes, hunting hares, or running far ahead.

"Only think," said Theras, "we have come half-way on our road to Athens and no mishaps."

"We got lost a lot of times," said Abas, who was afraid to be so happy.

"Yes, but we always found the way again. And those Spartans never even caught a glimpse of us."

"Be careful, be careful," said Abas. "The gods might hear you."

They were just passing a little shrine to Pan, who was the god of shepherds.

Theras stopped.

"Here," he said, "let's offer to Pan all the cakes that Leon gave us."

Abas, brought up in farmer thrift, would have liked to keep some for the morrow. He did get so hungry walking in the mountain air.

Theras lifted his hands high before the shrine, standing and looking up to the sky as the Greeks always did in prayer.

"Hear us, O Pan," he said. "Bring us safe to

Athens, and my mother will offer thee a gift ten times our little gift to-day."

After this they went on again, Theras still skipping and twirling above his head a light, sharp-pointed spear. For Leon had given Theras a spear and Abas a bow and arrows.

"Ye'll sure need 'em," he had said. "I don't see how ye ever came this far without a weapon. Just luck or the good gods!"

"It was Athena," Theras had answered. "I think she wants us back in Athens."

Leon would not have thought of giving Abas the spear and Theras the arrows. For he could see that Theras was a high-born lad. And among the Greeks, the high-born lads, or citizens, always had spears or swords, while the Perioikoi had arrows. This was just as well, for Abas had always used the bow, and Theras both in Athens and Sparta had practised hurling the lance. He little thought now what great need he would have of it.

CHAPTER LIV

Not a Pussy-Cat

Next day they were on their way to Mantinea, another Arkadian city. To go there was like climbing over the rough shoulder of the world. Higher and ever steeper were the mountains, and the roads were often but little sheep-paths.

And now Abas noticed that their path was getting narrower and fainter. They were so high up that the clouds were below them, rolling softly along like great white fleece.

"They are sheep, those clouds," laughed Theras, "and the wind is their shepherd driving them."

Abas did not answer. He was worried about the path.

Yes, it had disappeared completely. Only a sheep-track leading nowhere.

"We've taken the wrong turn," he said. "We must go down again."

"All right," said Theras cheerily.

They turned back and found another path, which they followed. But this path ended at a ruined hut. Back again they turned. They were now thoroughly mixed up. A cloud came along, wrapping the mountain as in a cloak. They could not see the sun which always had been their guide. And now evening was falling. Even Kairos kept sniffing around as if he knew they were not in the right place.

"We'd better not walk any more," said Abas. "We'll only go farther off the road. We'll have to spend the night here."

They had two small pieces of bread which they had saved from noon. These they ate.

"Oh, we'll be all right," said Theras. "I wish you'd shoot a hare. Only we haven't any way of making fire to cook him."

"No. I wish we had a flint," said Abas. "Father can make fire of two sticks, but he couldn't in this dampness." For the rocks were dripping in the mist. Their cloaks, as they wrapped themselves in them, were wet indeed.

But in spite of the dampness and cold the two boys were soon asleep, and Kairos snuggled close to them, growling every now and then.

Theras awoke before sunrise.

"Look, Abas," he cried out. "The clouds are breaking up and we can see everything. Let's go while we can see."

So up they got and went searching for the path. Abas forged ahead, hoping to shoot a hare. For perhaps they would come to a shepherd's hut where they could roast it. Both boys were ravenously hungry.

They were now in a deep glen overgrown with scrub oak and pine.

Suddenly the bushes crashed—once—twice. Kairos gave a frightened howl, and out leaped the biggest cat Theras had ever seen. She was like a house pussy —but big—so big and lithe! Her face, too, did not look like a house cat's. It was broad and cruel with heavy hairy jaws and the two eyes glared at Abas. She did not see Theras.

Abas turned quickly—saw her, but before he could shoot his arrow the cat had leaped upon him.

Abas dodged the claws and seized the cat's throat. But his strength was nothing against the hungry animal's.

All in a second Theras saw this. All in a second it came to him that he must throw his spear true and strong or Abas would be dead.

He lifted his spear and aimed just back of the cat's shoulder. Suddenly a man's strength seemed to flow into him, and he *hurled*.

Great Zeus! What a yowl! The wildcat sprang back, spun around and around, trying to bite the spear.

"Shoot, Abas, shoot!" yelled Theras.

And Abas snatched up his bow which had fallen in the shock, aimed as best he could, and shot. Think of it! He shot the wildcat in the eye. Of course, he was very close. Then leaving the beast still whirling about and howling, the boys ran and scrambled away.

"There may be another," called Theras. "Run, run!"

CHAPTER LV

Kindness in Arkadia

OUT of the glen they climbed, on to a great shoulder of mountain, running, running until their breath gave out and they could only pant along.

Theras pointed across a valley to another hill.

"What is that black spot?" he asked. "A hut, isn't it?"

Abas peered under his hand.

"Yes, it is."

So over stock and stone the two made for the hut.

About mid-morning they reached it. The shepherd and his wife were there. Much astonished they were at sight of two hungry boys in that wild place.

"Ye're far off the road," they exclaimed. "Where

be ye goin'? An' what is that awful cut on yer shoulder?"

For Abas had got a deep scratch from Mistress Wildcat.

They were very kind, the shepherd and his wife. They washed Abas's wound. "She'd been prowlin' all night, that beast," said the man, "and got naught. That's what made her so fierce."

The woman gave the boys a good breakfast. Then the man went out with them to find the spear, the arrow, and their cloaks, all of which they had left. Theras could never have found the way back, but Abas had watched the way.

They found the cat near the same place, dead. "Artemis save us," said the man. "It's a young lynx. Look at her stubby tail and her jaw whiskers." He drew out the spear.

"A good shot that," said he, at which Theras was proud.

Then they skinned the lynx, and went back to the shepherd's hut.

Next morning they started out once more, making resolutions to watch the road every moment.

"But ye can meet wildcats an' bears, too, on the best road up here around," said the shepherd. "It's no place for two boys alone."

In spite of this dire warning Theras and Abas made their way with difficulty, but no actual dangers, past Alea and the little town of Philius and on to Corinth.

It was after Corinth that they met their worst danger, and then not from beast but from man.

CHAPTER LVI

A Dangerous Inn

THE shepherds and farmers in the region of Corinth were not so kind. Often and often Theras and Abas went hungry. Once they were refused the house. But this was rare in Greece, where being kind to strangers was the one good deed which the gods rewarded first, before everything else.

They had reached Corinth in the afternoon and had gone on by it, and at nightfall they came to a sort of inn, where the landlord was at first very gruff but then suddenly relented and let them enter.

The inn was a stone building of two stories. The boys were put on the upper floor. It was the first time Abas had ever gone upstairs.

"That's nothing," boasted Theras. "We have stairs at home, and soon we'll be there." He gave a hop of delight.

Theras, as usual, had done all the talking. For Abas, as he came far from home, grew timid and shy. But though Theras had talked he could hardly understand the landlord of the inn, he spoke such an outlandish jargon. Greek it was, but a queer, coarse Greek, from some Ægean island probably. For men came to Corinth from all places and ports.

The two boys spread their cloaks on the floor and sat down to eat their supper which fortunately they had brought with them. Theras was humming as he ate and throwing scraps to Kairos who took them at one gulp.

But Abas laid his hand on Theras with a "Hush, listen!"

A company of men had come into the inn below and were drinking and talking.

"I can't understand a word," said Theras.

"I can," said Abas, white as a stone. He listened with horrified face.

"They are saying," said Abas, "that they will take us for slaves. The landlord wants to seize us now, but the other man says we can't get out, so wait till morning."

Theras jumped to his feet.

"No use," moaned Abas. "There's no way out but down the stairs into the midst of them."

Theras looked at the one window. It was above their heads. The place certainly looked like a prison.

Theras cautiously bolted the door.

"It's no use," whispered Abas. "It's a trap. We're like rabbits caught."

Abas's chin was trembling so he could scarcely speak.

Still Theras kept looking around.

"No, we mustn't be caught," he muttered.

The room was utterly bare save for a sea-chest in one corner.

"Help me carry this," he whispered. "Quiet! Don't make a noise."

Abas took one handle and, staggering under the weight, the two boys carried the chest to the window.

A DANGEROUS INN

"But we're too high up," said Abas almost angrily. "Can't you see we can't jump?"

Theras mounted upon the chest and looked out. Yes, though it was dark, he could see that the hill fell away below the window and the ground was rough. There was a wall around the inn, but oh, kind gods, the small gate was ajar!

Suddenly Theras jumped from the chest, and picking up his cloak tied the corner of it to Abas's cloak in a hard sailor knot. For Athenian boys were taught sailor ways. These cloaks were not shaped at all. They were just large squares of woven cloth. Theras now tied another corner to the thick handles of the chest and the cloaks became something like a long, thick rope, which now he flung over the window-sill.

Abas caught his breath with sudden light and hope. "Yes, yes," he said.

"I'll go first," said Theras, "and you hand me down Kairos and my spear. Then follow like lightning."

As he spoke he climbed upon the chest, pulled himself up astride the window-ledge, and looked out.

Yes, the inn yard was deserted and the men inside were singing over their wine.

With a prayer to Athena, Theras swung himself out, and, clinging with legs and arms to the thick cloaks, let himself down. Before Theras touched the ground Abas had reached down the spear and dog and then, with his own bow and arrows strapped to his back, Abas came down by the cloaks.

CHAPTER LVII

A Wilderness

CAUTIOUSLY a-tiptoe, the boys made their way across the inn yard and out of the gate. Then they began to run like mad through the low pine wood. It was dreadful going, over sharp rocks and gullies.

"Come! This way," panted Theras.

And turning toward the high-road they went across it and down the other side.

"They'd hunt for us in the wood," he panted. "We must go along the cliff."

So they crept, climbed, or hurried, as the lay of the land allowed them, along the outer cliff. The high-road was above them. Below them at the foot of the crags was the sea, washing and splashing. The stars were bright and the reflection of the sea showed them the way. They followed the high-road, and at times the cliff was so steep that they had to climb back again to the road for a space. But they always left it again for fear of the slave-dealers.

Suddenly Abbas took a miserable tumble among the crags. Theras looked back to see him get up again. But instead he doubled in a heap, rocking to and fro. Theras ran to him.

"Abas, what is it? You must get up, you must!"

"Yes, yes," answered Abas, "I will. I hurt my ankle."

He got up carefully. But each time he put his left foot to the ground he could not repress a cry of pain.

Theras put one arm about Abas and again they went forward, Abas limping terribly.

Neither boy said a word. They knew they must keep on going or be caught.

"Come up to the high-road," said Theras. "It's deserted. We can get along better."

So for an hour, keeping careful look-out, they limped along the road. Abas groaned now and then, but when he groaned he only pushed on faster. On and on!

Then without any warning Abas doubled into a limp heap. Theras just saved him from falling flat.

"What is it? Abas! Abas!"

But Abas did not answer. In the pale light of the moon which had just appeared, Abas's face looked as white as chalk.

Theras shook him, called him. He did not know what to do. He began to cry with pity.

"Abas, I didn't mean to make you walk so fast! Abas, Abas! I didn't know it was hurting you like that."

Kairos ran up and licked Abas's face, whining and crying too.

But now quietly Abas opened his eyes and looked about for a moment.

Then his face twitched as the pain came rushing back.

"Come," he said, scrambling up, but again he tumbled down. "My head whirls," said Abas. "I—— I—— Theras, don't you wait for me. Go on, please, go on. I'll catch up with you."

F

"I won't go on," said Theras.

He began to feel Abas's ankle, but Abas shuddered at the touch.

"Look here, Abas," said Theras suddenly, "I'll carry you."

"No, no, you mustn't do that. You can't, Theras. It will only——"

"Stop struggling and help," said Theras. "I'm going to carry you."

He stooped down. "Get on my back," he commanded. "No words. *Do it!*"

And Abas got upon Theras's back with arms about his neck.

"You don't weigh anything," said Theras. "Great Zeus! This is a lot easier."

Certainly Theras could go faster now. He jogged along the road, speaking every now and then a cheery word to Abas. The little crooked moon rose higher over the sea. And then grey dawn began and the sea grew all strangely white.

But Abas seemed to grow heavier and heavier. He really weighed nearly as much as Theras.

Theras was thankful now for the Spartan training, that training which built up a boy's strength day after day and taught him to go on even after the muscles seemed spent and worn out.

Morning came at last. Theras found a good hiding-place among the rocks by a little waterfall. He let Abas down, stretched his aching self on the rocks, and went to sleep like a falling star.

CHAPTER LVIII

THE BURDEN UPON THERAS

It was afternoon when Theras awoke. There was Abas washing his ankle at the stream. Past all semblance of ankle was it swollen, and black half-way to the knee. Abas's face looked white and drawn.

"Look over in the bushes," he said. "I shot a squirrel while I was waiting for you to wake up. He came quite close because we were so still. But I could not fetch him."

Theras searched and, sure enough, the squirrel was there. Abas helped him to skin it and Theras after much trouble started a fire by using two sharp stones and some dry moss. Abas meanwhile had cut the squirrel into pieces, and so they roasted him on the end of a long stick.

How ravenously they ate! And by the time they finished the sun had sunk so that they could go on again.

Theras scrambled up to reconnoitre the road just in time to see a company of rough men coming toward him. He hid until they had passed and then went back to Abas.

"We mustn't use the road," he said. "The rocks here are pretty good." And he helped Abas upon his back.

He knew only too well that they were nearing the

Skironian Rocks, where the Spartans had met the robbers and where the woods and rocks were famous for robber bands.

"But those rough robbers would not want us," said Abas. "They want to steal goods."

"They'd steal us quick enough," answered Theras. "We'd bring them more money than bales of goods."

So with difficult steps Theras made his way along the rocks, resting when he had to rest, and setting Abas down, then pushing onward again.

He wished he were as agile as Kairos, who seemed able to get footing anywhere.

As night deepened the cliffs became so steep that Theras was forced to go back to the road. But now even the road was steep uphill. Abas seemed to weigh like a grown man and Theras's breath came pantingly. Thankful was he when dawn came and again he slept. That day Theras looked for a bird, rabbit, or squirrel to shoot, but he found none. He did not dare to go too far from Abas for fear of losing him.

That night, faint with hunger and spent with effort, Theras once more got Abas upon his back. Abas had protested and tried to walk, but it was no use. The faintness returned and Abas reeled like a man drunk with wine.

"Besides," said Theras, "you don't make any headway. It's just creeping."

But the night went badly. Again and again Theras had to put Abas down, panting as he rested. Then after midnight, just as he gained the top of the hill, Theras's knees suddenly buckled under him. They bent like blades of grass, and both he and Abas fell headlong on the road.

CHAPTER LIX

A Sorrowful Pass

WHEN they got themselves untangled, there was Abas rubbing his poor foot that had taken an extra wrench, and Theras clasping his knees which kept quivering and shaking. Something inside his chest kept shaking too, and trying to make him cry.

Abas nodded his head savagely.

"Theras, son of Pheidon, now you've hurt me again," he said.

"I'm sorry," said Theras.

"You shall not carry me," went on Abas, "you shall not. Not one step farther, not one step."

"I will," snapped Theras with quivering lip.

"No, by Hermes. I'm only keeping you back so both of us will die. I can take my chance. You take yours. You go right on and I'll——"

"Abas, if you thought I was that kind of boy, why did you come with me?"

"You can't help it. You—you—— I tell you, Theras. I won't get on your back again, never!" Abas's voice sounded very queer.

"I promised Baukis I'd save you, and I'm going to do it," spoke Theras. "So you needn't say anything about it."

"The gods meant me to die or they wouldn't have hurt my ankle," said Abas.

"Nonsense! If the gods broke your ankle it was to see if you had the grit to go on."

"I've got grit. I'm a Spartan!"

"No, you are not. You're going to be an Athenian now, and you're coming with me."

"I won't."

"You will."

Both boys were half crying now in their quarrel.

Theras got up on his shaking legs.

"I'll hit you, Abas," he sputtered. "You're only insulting me after—after I've tried—to—— I tell you I *can* carry you."

He staggered toward Abas as if to carry out his threat, but Abas put up his hands pitifully.

"The old black ewe can carry me," he said. "You don't need to, Theras."

"The old black ewe!" repeated Theras, stopping short.

"Yes, our Œta over there." Abas pointed to a black rock. "She can carry me well, but Mother must give us soup before we start. She's *stingy* not to give soup when we are so hungry, so hungry—so hungry!"

Theras stared at Abas's face. It was terribly red through its dust and dirt, and his eyes glittered strangely. Not like Abas at all.

A cold fear struck through Theras.

"Abas," he pleaded, "there isn't any ewe. Your mother isn't there."

But Abas only kept muttering, "Hungry, hungry!"

Now Theras knew. Abas was very ill. Might he not die then and there on the rocks? How terrible to hear him saying words which meant nothing—muttering like that.

All the quivering went out of Theras's knees. He began to stand up straight. He looked around.

"I must get him something to eat," he said aloud. "I must."

They had not seen any hut all night, and even if he did come to a hut would Theras dare to go to it after what had happened at the inn?

Theras picked up the bow and arrow and hurried down into a glen where the few low bushes might hide rabbit or squirrel or bird. He crept along searching, searching. But the air appeared full of mist. And sometimes Theras seemed strangely to forget what he was looking for.

Up another hill he climbed—peeped over a crest of rocks.

By Hermes, there was the high-road, and yes, in the distance, a company of men coming!

Theras instantly ran back and hid behind some bushes. But the bushes seemed lonely, the rocks a terror. He longed to see the men again. It was dreadful to be alone.

He crept back to the rock where he could peep at them. He knew it was foolish to do this. They might see and catch him.

Oh, but what if they should be *good* men—not robbers at all! If they were good they would save Abas. Theras would not have to see him die out there alone.

He watched the men as they came near—nearer. Almost under his rock they stopped, took out a huge basket of food, and sat down to eat.

Oh, Zeus, how Theras did want that bread, that cheese and roast fowl! Even so far away he seemed to smell them—what fragrance! He could not stand it.

Theras crept down the hill nearer to the men. He could hear them laughing—joking.

How like home it sounded to hear men talking freely like that.

Then one man came and sat a little distance from the rest. He lifted something glittering—a lyre, surely a lyre.

Oh, Athena preserve us! The man was singing.

Without one prudent thought more, Theras half ran, half stumbled down the rocks, bursting out from the bushes like a scared partridge.

He leaped to the man, throwing both arms around the man's knee. For that was the Greek way of "supplication," or asking in great need.

CHAPTER LX

HERODOTOS

"GREAT thundering Zeus!"

The man dropped his lyre and caught it only by one string.

"What do you want, you rogue? Let go. Let go."

"Help me! Help Abas," stammered Theras, hardly able to speak for sobs that kept getting in his way.

A slave rushed forward and dragged Theras back.

"A decoy, master," he said. "The robbers oft send forth a boy like this. Ho, there; your swords, men!"

This brought Theras to his senses.

"I am not a decoy," he cried out clearly. "An Athenian boy wouldn't help robbers. Oh, can't you see I am Athenian?"

How Theras thought anyone could see he was an Athenian, a gentleman's son, I cannot imagine. There he was—dirty face, tangled hair, his chiton half torn off him, and he himself thin as a long-legged crane.

But the man with the lyre had sense.

"Let the boy go, Jason," he commanded. "Come here, son." He took Theras's trembling hand. "Now tell me who you are."

Theras kept trying to keep back the sobs.

"I am Pheidon's son, in Athens. They took me away, but I am going back."

"Great Zeus—alone?"

*F

"No, no, Abas is with me. And Abas is *dying* up there among the rocks. Oh, come quick and save him. Come! It doesn't matter so much about me."

"I told you," spoke the slave. "The child is from the robbers. He wants to get us up there into a trap."

Theras could not answer. He was too frightened. He only looked up into the master's eyes, pleading like a dog to be trusted. What deep blue eyes they were that met his! What kind, wise eyes, not smiling but always as if about to smile. They seemed to look Theras through and through. Suddenly the blue eyes filled with tears.

"Look here, gentlemen," said the man, turning to the others of the party who had crowded about. "I trust this boy if you do not. Who'll come with me to find this friend of his?"

"I will."

"And I."

"I too," spoke some young man.

The man took Theras's hand and, the others following, they mounted the rocks from which Theras had come.

At first Theras could not see the little glen where he had hunted rabbits. He was so eager to make the men believe him that it made him confused and uncertain. But even so his new friend did not think Theras a liar.

"Take your time," he said. "You will soon remember the path."

Then Theras spied the glen. And from that he knew his way back to Abas. Now he caught sight of Abas lying like a heap of rags and ran ahead of the men. He knelt down—lifted Abas's head.

"Abas, Abas, I have found someone to help. Listen to me. Don't keep talking!"

But Abas only tossed his head from side to side, muttering:

"Hungry, hungry, hungry!"

Oh, what a wonderful thing to see Abas lifted in the arms of the kind stranger and carried down to the road! To see the stranger giving Abas milk and binding up his ankle with some strong-smelling, healing herbs.

And Theras, too, had bread and cheese and roast chicken to eat.

Surely it was a dream and no truth!

Then the slaves laid Abas on a rude litter, to carry him along the road. And thus the party started forward.

But now the kind man stood beside Theras and lifted him in his arms as if he had been a small child.

"You are not strong enough to walk," said the kind voice. "Jason and I will carry you, my brave Athenian."

Theras put his arms about the man's neck. At that moment he felt that he loved him more than anyone in the world.

"Who are you?" he asked wonderingly.

"I am Herodotos," he answered. "I used to know your father in Athens."

CHAPTER LXI

THE MAN WHO KNEW ALL THE WONDERS OF THE WORLD

BUT Herodotos was wrong. Theras was soon strong enough to walk with the others.

By the time they were approaching Megara he was almost himself again. Whether it was the good food, the feeling of safety after the long danger, seeing Abas lying so comfortable on his litter, already opening his eyes sensibly, or the surety of getting to Athens, I do not know. Perhaps it was all these things. But most of all I think it was the laughing talk and the music by the way.

For Herodotos could play such merry marching tunes.

If you were ever on a long, weary tramp so that you could hardly press one yard farther, and then someone has started singing in good rhythm, you will know what I mean. Immediately your legs begin to move and your shoulders straighten. You forget your tiredness.

To Theras this was even greater refreshment, for these were the old marching tunes of Athens which Theras had always known.

And Herodotos told the most marvellous stories that Theras (or any other boy in the world, for that matter) had ever heard.[1] He told of Egypt, where the rain never falls, but where a great river overflows and waters all the land. He told of the tombs of kings, great pyramids which looked like real mountains where gods might live. He told of a wonderful black bird like a crane which could fight with serpents and conquer them, and of an animal which, hatching from an egg the size of a goose egg, grew to be eight feet long.

"It hath the eyes of a pig," said Herodotos. "Teeth large, like tusks, and no tongue at all. And it can move its upper jaw but not the lower. Try now whether you can do the same."

And Theras and Abas tried their best to move their mouths that way, but only fell to laughing at the funny faces they made

And oh, the stories of kings and heroes that Herodotos knew! Cyrus, who as a baby was cast out upon a mountain-side to die, yet found his way to his throne. The tyrant Periander, who lost his ring in the sea but found it again in a fish which they brought him for dinner.

And Herodotos himself—what a tall, gallant man! His beard was touched with grey, but how swiftly he moved, as if he could never grow old, and there was not the smallest thing by the roadside, herb or animal or wayside shrine, but Herodotos knew all about it. You had only to ask him the question.

Theras would walk for hours with his hand in his.

---

[1] Herodotos wrote all these stories in a book which is yet with us and which you can read.

He was afraid to walk ahead for fear he would lose something Herodotos was saying. And the strange part of it was, the grown men of the party listened with as much interest as the little boy.

"Who told you all those things?" asked Theras wonderingly. For there were no books which told of these facts.

"Men in Egypt, men in Ionia, men in Persia, in Italy, and in the Garden of Hesperides," answered Herodotos. "But best of all my own eyes looked and saw."

"But have you been so far, to so many lands?"

"Yes, child, and to many others. I never weary of this world in which we live."

CHAPTER LXII

THE BAY OF SALAMIS

Now they came to the Bay of Salamis. And here Herodotos did something most wonderful of all. He began to tell them the story of how the Persians came—millions of men—to fight Greece, who had only hundreds.

He told of the assembling of ships in Salamis Bay—triremes with three banks of oars on either side, penticonters, sailing ships of all sorts, and ships with beaks afront to ram the enemy. There were the ships of Athens, of Ægina, Corinth, Megara, and Sparta. He told the number each city sent. But Athens had sent the most.

THE BAY OF SALAMIS

Here in Salamis Bay the ships awaited the enormous fleet of the Persians and all Asia to come upon them.

Herodotos pointed out where each ship had waited, until Theras could fairly see the gallant line of them, white and fluttering on the blue of Salamis Bay, and even Abas sat up on his litter to look over the landlocked harbour.

Theras's own grandfathers, both of them, had been in those ships and in that fight.

"And on that hill yonder," said Herodotos, now chanting his story almost like a song, "sat the Persian king Xerxes, waiting to see his ships chase the Grecian ships and destroy them."

Theras began to prance and clap his hands, for he knew well the Persian king's disappointment.

"Now they came, those Persian ships, whitening all the water like a flock of gulls—everywhere, everywhere ships! They entered the bay, a fearful multitude, and attacked at once.

"The Greeks were frightened and began to back water with their oars.

"But Athena came like a great form of mist above the ships and said:

"'Why do ye back water, O Greeks? Why are ye afraid?'

"Then one of the Athenian captains named Amenias darted his ship forth in front of the line and charged the leading ship of the Persians."

"Well done, Amenias!" shouted Theras. He knew Amenias's son at school.

"Yes, well done, Amenias," Herodotos went on,

"for by his courage he began the battle in the right way.

"Soon the two vessels became entangled. Then out flew all the rest of the Greek ships to help Amenias. Then hither and yon the battle raged in the narrow strait. So narrow were the waters that the Persians had little good of their many ships. The ships were too crowded and fell foul of each other. And in the fighting they were all confusion—everywhere, anywhere. But our ships fought in order. We kept our line. We were skilled sailors and cool in our fighting. No wonder we vanquished the Persian."

So walking beside the blue, quiet, and peaceful bay, the boys with that master story-teller, Herodotos, fought all over again the Battle of Salamis, until the Persians were in flight and the wrecks of their ships scattered on the shore, as the gods had foretold.

CHAPTER LXIII

Coming Home

By this time they were come to Eleusis. Now Theras could not think of past glories or Salamis battles or anything else, except that he was only four miles from Athens. Every time he thought of it his heart gave a great jump, and as he thought of it every minute, his heart was always jumping. He ran eagerly ahead of the party, hurrying all alone with his joy.

COMING HOME

When they reached Aigaleos Theras ran until he reached the hill-top.

For here, blessed wonder, he saw Athens itself like a dream of a city in the violet, misty distance. Yes, there was the wall, the little crowded houses within it, and the Akropolis with its temples guarding all.

But Theras saw more than this earthly part of Athens. For out from Athens seemed to look the face of his goddess who was always there—Athena!

Her face was like that which he had seen long ago in the Parthenon temple when the morning sun had struck upon the golden dress of the image and reflected up into the rose-hued, living face of her. The heavenly face of Athena had entered then the heart of the little boy. And it had never left it. Now he saw it even more alive, larger, smiling as the heavens seem to smile before the sunrise. Happy the boy who could see his goddess so plain.

When Herodotos came up to the hill-top he saw Theras standing there, head up, lips apart, as if he were drinking the happiness of home.

But as the party joined them with merry talk and laughing voices, Theras ran to Abas.

"Look, look!" he cried. "There is the Akropolis and the temples on it. And down in that part of the city where you see the market-square is my home. It will be your home too, Abas. Oh, what would Baukis say now? We are really here!"

They entered the Dipylon Gate of Athens in the soft, golden sunset hour.

It was the sixth day of the Panathenaic Festival,

the greatest day of all the Athenian year. The streets were thronged with gaily-dressed people, laughing, calling merrily to one another, all hurrying homeward, hither and yon. Splendid young men on horseback wound in among them, proudly smiling, having ridden in the great Panathenaic Procession. The altars everywhere were decked with flowers. O happy, god-beloved city! Wonderful Athens!

Herodotos looked about him regretfully.

"Ah, we should have reached here this morning," he said. "We have missed the great procession and 'giving of the robe.'"

Herodotos did not say that taking up two forlorn, travel-weary boys by the wayside had caused the delay.

"Now, my son," he said, "I must go to the house of the council."

"Not to your own house?" queried Theras.

"No, I do not live in Athens now," replied Herodotos, and his face looked sad as he said it. He added:

"Abas shall be carried along with you. I shall see you to-morrow. Are you sure you do not need me now?"

"Oh, no—no, thank you," said Theras, hardly able to answer, so eager was he to hurry home.

And yet how slowly he had to go beside Abas's litter! They passed through the market-place. Men hurried by them, carrying bundles of sacrificial meat from the generous sacrifice on the Akropolis. Everyone, even the very poor, would feast to-night at home or with friends. Ah, here was the very booth where Father had bought the dolls for Aglaia and Opis.

Suddenly the memory of Pheidon, his strong splendid Father, came clearly upon Theras, clearly and with painful sorrow. No happy Athenaic feast would bring Father back, as in the old days, at the head of the table. This Athenaic feast was the nearest to Christmas merriment that an Athenian boy could know.

But Father would not be there.

Theras bowed his head to hide his tears, for Abas would certainly wonder at them.

Oh, here was the Kerameikos Quarter and now the *street,* his very street. How like, yet how different it looked. Theras knew every corner, every turn, every roof, and there was Theras's home.

He ran ahead—he could not help it—seized the beloved latch, and flung open his own home door.

But a strange doorkeeper met him!

"Hi, hi, you young thief! What do you mean - opening my door? Why didn't you knock?"

CHAPTER LXIV

STRANGERS EVERYWHERE

"WHERE is Mother?" demanded Theras, trying to push past the porter slave. "Mother — I mean Arethusa. Where is she?"

"Not here, young rogue. Arethusa has not lived here for a year past, as well you know."

"Not lived here? Where is she? What do you mean?"

Theras's distress was so plain that the door slave took pity.

"I don't know where she is, my boy. I really don't," he said.

"But who lives here?"

"Why, my master, of course, Dion."

Theras could hardly speak for anger and wonder and sudden grief.

"How did he get my house?"

"He bought it from Metion."

"It isn't his house; it is mine. I am Pheidon's son."

"All the same, Metion sold it and took Arethusa away to live at his home."

Theras remembered only vaguely where his cousin Metion lived. Pheidon's family had never liked him nor exchanged visits with him.

Without a word Theras ran to the next door, thumping it loudly. The neighbours would tell him where his mother and little sisters were gone.

But the neighbours were all out attending the Panathenaic Festival. Even the women went out to-day. Theras knocked at the next door—the next.

The slaves, hurrying, busy with the extra cooking, did not know where Arethusa had gone.

Theras stood in a daze. Suddenly the familiar street was a wilderness more dreary than Arkadia or the Skironian Rocks. Home had always contained Mother. Now here was home and Mother gone. The whole world was upside down.

Abas sat up on his litter.

"Can't you find anybody? I'll help you, Theras. I can walk a little now."

Theras could hardly bring himself back to answer.

"No, Abas, you would only hurt your foot, and you would be slow. Oh, I must run, run till I find her!"

He longed to be free and alone.

The litter slaves spoke:

"Master, we can take Abas back to our master, Herodotos. Then you can go and search."

The slaves knew perfectly well that they should not leave Theras alone. But they were hungry for their supper.

"Yes, yes," said Theras. "Take him to Herodotos. I will come after—after I find her."

But in his heart he did not hope to find Arethusa. This was too strange and dreadful. To be in Athens where all should be joy, and to find only sorrow.

Alone in the twilight he turned down the narrow street. Whither should he go? His first thought was of course his school, and so he hurried thither. The boys would be gone at this hour, but the master lived next door.

He soon reached the little open portico—his school. The same seats, the same lyres hanging on the wall, and the scattered tablets.

But all was deserted. He knocked next door, but got no response at all. No doubt the master, too, was at the festival.

Theras turned aimlessly. He did not think of looking for Herodotos. He thought only of Arethusa and that he could not, *could not* find her.

He came to the foot of the Akropolis. Here all the air smelt of myrrh and frankincense from the many sacrifices. Dense crowds were still swarming down the marble staircase, flower crowned, weary with merry-making. But in the confusion and growing darkness Theras saw nobody he knew. Dreadful it is to be lonely in a crowd where everyone is laughing and jostling about.

Theras turned right-about, trying to get away from them. The streets no longer looked familiar. Now he unexpectedly found himself in the market-place again. Market had long been over, and the place was littered and dirty. Some public slaves were cleaning up, and over in one corner a man was standing idly, his back to Theras.

Theras dragged himself over to ask his question. That back! He had seen it before, and that thatch of black hair!

"Can you tell me——" he began.

The man turned.

Great luck of Olympians! It was Lampon! Lampon and no other!

Theras stretched up his arms to him, as he used to do when a tiny boy.

"Lampon, oh, Lampon! Where is Mother? Take me to Mother!"

Lampon jumped straight up in the air and began muttering enchantments:

> "Mumbly Thumbly winky wee,
> Save me from the ghost I see."

Something of that sort, anyhow, Lampon said.

But Theras caught at his skirt and Lampon had to know he was real.

Then how Lampon hugged him and kissed him! "Little master, little master!" he kept saying. "Oh, where did ye come from? However did ye get here? O joyful day!" But Lampon did not wait to hear the answers. He was too happy.

CHAPTER LXV

Real Home

"Surely, surely do I know where Arethusa is. Stayin' at Epikides's house since that villain Metion put us out. We'll have the law on him. So we will."

Even in his joy Theras wondered how they could have the law without Father to see to it.

Lampon caught Theras's hand and pulled him breathlessly out of the market-place and along the dark street.

They stopped by a doorway, bright-lighted for the evening feast. Theras saw the guests arriving, someone greeting them.

Suddenly Theras cried out in such amaze that his cry sounded like terror. For the man greeting the guests was *his own father, Pheidon*, as alive as anybody could be. Now it was Theras's turn to think he was seeing a ghost.

Pheidon turned at Theras's cry and with a gasp caught sight of his boy in the doorway.

"Theras, Theras!" he cried. He strode toward Theras, dropped on his knees with outstretched arms, and into those arms Theras ran as to the dearest haven in the world. All the room seemed bright and alight with the sudden joy.

"Where did you come from, child? How did you get here?" Pheidon was asking.

"But you were dead, Father, you were dead," sobbed Theras foolishly.

Oh, the hearty, well-remembered laugh—Father's laugh!

"Don't I seem alive?"

For answer Theras only clung closer and suddenly, in those arms, it did not seem strange for Pheidon to be alive. Death had been strange, but not this warm familiar life.

"I was a prisoner in Samos," explained Pheidon. "I and a score of others were thought dead, and so they told it in Athens. But we are all safe home again."

"And Mother. Where is Mother?" asked Theras.

"Wait, son, she has had the great surprise of my coming home, and now this. Wait until I tell her."

Pheidon rose, then stooped to kiss Theras again before he could go. Then he disappeared into the inner court, while Theras obediently waited.

He heard the low speech, the dear kind voice telling, then a sudden, sharp, painful cry—his mother's.

"Where? Where is Theras?"

Theras could be obedient no longer. He ran leaping into the court and straight to his mother's embrace.

Then indeed was such a laughing, kissing, crying, and broken words trying to tell what had happened in those sorrowful months past as would have warmed the coldest heart.

Aglaia came in and even little Opis was awakened out of her sleep and carried in. She was ever so much bigger than when Theras had gone away. But she did not quite remember her big brother and was half frightened by all the commotion about her.

For you will have seen that the Athenians were not quiet people, but full of enthusiasm, both in sorrow and in joy.

Maro came shyly in to join the family happiness, and kind Arethusa drew him to her, telling what a comfort the adopted son had been to her while the real son was away. For a moment Theras was jealous of his foster-brother.

"But how did you come back, son?" asked Pheidon. "I was making ready to go to Sparta to fetch you."

"I didn't know that, Father. I ran away—I and another boy. We went up into Arkadia."

"All that way—just two boys alone? That long road back to Athens?"

There were both wonder and pride in Pheidon's voice. "Great Athena, you might have been killed a hundred times!"

"We were almost," said Theras.

And then what delight to tell all the dangers of the journey, the chase of the Spartans, the faithful Perioikoi, the wildcat, the treacherous innkeeper, and poor Abas's sprained ankle.

"But did Abas get here?" Pheidon's face suddenly darkened with displeasure. "My son, surely you did not leave him by the way?"

"No, Father, I carried him."

"Great Zeus! All the way?"

"No, because at last I fell down and could not get up."

Arethusa's arm stole about Theras, drawing him to her. Pheidon said no praise, but Theras could see the praise shining in his face.

How good it was to be at home!

"But where is the Spartan boy now?" asked Pheidon.

"He's with Herodotos. Oh, Herodotos saved us on the road, Father, and oh, he knows everything, Herodotos does."

Pheidon laughed merrily.

"Herodotos! I should think so. That's the greatest piece of luck I ever heard of. Fell in with Herodotos, did you? Did he tell you any stories?"

"Oh, Father, the most wonderful stories, and— and——"

Pheidon laughed again.

"Stories—he couldn't help it," Pheidon said. "Herodotos will stop day or night to hear a story or to tell one. Herodotos is writing a book about our fight with the Persians. It is a wise and great book. Long after we are dead, men will read that book and know the deeds that were done."

CHAPTER LXVI

The Owl Mark

LATE as it was, that night Pheidon and Theras had to go over to the council house to see Herodotos and to make sure that Abas was safe.

Here while the boys were talking together, as if they had been parted a month, Herodotos in a low voice told Pheidon how he had found Theras, and how the boy had carried his friend until he had literally dropped in the road.

"I wish you had seen him when he came up to me," said Herodotos. "A wreck of a boy. And even then thinking of his friend Abas rather than himself. Would that I had such a son."

And Pheidon thanked the gods for his.

It was next day before Theras noted something which Pheidon had been dreading for him to speak of, namely, a terrible scar on Pheidon's forehead.

"What is it, Father?" questioned Theras. "Like a deep burn which has healed."

"What does it look like?" asked Pheidon.

"Father, it's strange, but it looks—it really does look like an *owl*."

"What about Epikides?" asked Pheidon, nodding toward his friend who was in the room.

To Theras's astonishment Epikides's forehead had the same scar, a deep-seared owl.

"Theras," said Pheidon sadly, "your father used to be a handsome man, but alas, he will never be so again."

Theras did not know what to say, for to an Athenian it was indeed a sorrow to have a mutilated face.

"But how did you get it, Father—that scar?"

"We were storming the walls of Samos," said Pheidon. "And all unexpected the Samians sallied forth from a hidden gate and surrounded us and then made for the ship.

"The ship pulled up anchor, leaving us undefended, and our whole band was taken prisoners. So the Samians kept us. They said that if Athens killed any of their men they would surely kill us. But all Athens thought we were already dead. And so they told here when they came home.

"At last peace was declared.

"Then the Samians took us into a prison room and brought red-hot searing irons with the owl picture upon them and branded our foreheads."

Theras winced with the pain which he seemed to be feeling himself.

"Yes," said Pheidon, "I thought my eyes would go out with the pain and fever of it, but thank the gods, my eyes recovered."

"But why did they make it an owl?" asked Theras.

"Because, son, the owl, as you know, is Athena's bird. They branded us as Athenians."

Theras thought of this awhile. His face brightened. "But after all, it's good to be marked for an Athenian," he said. "If you were lost in the wilderness as I was, everyone who met you—every single traveller—would know you are an Athenian."

"Well said, by Hermes, well said!" broke in Epikides.

"The Athenians honour us for it," he added. "After all, these are our battle scars."

CHAPTER LXVII

Good-bye

AND now the story of Theras is ended. There remains only to tell how Pheidon faithfully gave to the gods all the thank-offerings which Theras had promised on his journey.

He offered gifts to Athena on the Akropolis, and to Pan in the little cave in the side of the Akropolis Rock devoted to the goat-legged god. He also gave gifts to the merry little stream, Kiphissos, which Theras crossed just as he left Athens.

So he made good all the promises his son had made. He was a faithful and pious Athenian.

Then also I must tell you how Pheidon sued his cousin Metion and won back his home and his lands.

And what a happy morning was that when all the family and the slaves went back into the old home. For Pheidon's people had lived in that house for hundreds of years.

Theras grew up to be a brave Athenian and he fought in the Peloponnesian War, a sad war in which nobody won and everybody was worsted, which too often is the case.

But Abas did not become an Athenian. Herodotos took a fancy to so good a lad, and learning his story from Theras, he adopted Abas and took him out to his western home in Thurii, Italy.

Here Abas could become a full citizen, not merely a freed-man. Abas became a mariner and sailed all his life on the great Ægean and Adriatic Seas.

Many times in after years, though the Spartans did not know it, a western colonist landed on the south shore of Laconia and came up to Amyklai. There this colonist sought out an old couple and gave them all they could desire. But what they liked most among his gifts was the love and devotion of a son—their Abas who was their pride and joy.

And when Abas landed at Athens there was always a welcome awaiting him and an Athenian home flung open to receive him.

For the friendship of Abas and Theras, begun in hardships, lasted all through their lives.

THE END

Made At The
Temple Press
Letchworth
Great Britain

CPSIA information can be obtained
at www.ICGtesting.com
Printed in the USA
LVHW011546170821
695509LV00004B/312